Fortress • 55

Cathar Castles

Fortresses of the Albigensian Crusade
1209–1300

Marcus Cowper · Illustrated by Peter Dennis

Series editors Marcus Cowper and Nikolai Bogdanovic

First published in 2006 by Osprey Publishing

Midland House, West Way, Botley, Oxford OX2 0PH, UK

443 Park Avenue South, New York, NY 10016, USA

E-mail: info@ospreypublishing.com

ISBN 10: 1 84603 066 8

ISBN 13: 978 1 84603 066 6

Design: Ken Vail Graphic Design, Cambridge, UK

Typeset in Monotype Gill Sans and ITC Stone Serif

Cartography: Map Studio, Romsey, UK/John Richards

Index by Alison Worthington

Originated by United Graphics, Singapore

Printed in China through Bookbuilders

06 07 08   10 9 8 7 6 5 4 3 2 1

A CIP catalogue record for this book is available from the British Library.

FOR A CATALOGUE OF ALL BOOKS PUBLISHED BY OSPREY MILITARY AND AVIATION PLEASE CONTACT:

Osprey Direct, c/o Random House Distribution Center, 400 Hahn Road, Westminster, MD 21157

Email: info@ospreydirect.com

Osprey Direct UK, P.O. Box 140, Wellingborough, Northants, NN8 2FA, UK

E-mail: info@ospreydirect.co.uk

www.ospreypublishing.com

Dedication

In memory of my father, Christopher Pennington Cowper (19 June 1936–15 September 2005).

Acknowledgements

I would like to acknowledge the help of the following people and institutions in obtaining images for this publication: Nikolai Bogdanovic; Xavier Beaujard, Chargé de Communication of the Communauté de Communes de la Piège et du Lauragais; AKG-images; and the British Library. I am also very grateful to Peter Dennis for painting the wonderful artwork plates that adorn this title, Richard and Hazel Watson of The Map Studio for creating the maps, and John Richards for drawing the line artwork.

I would like to thank Anita Canonica-Battaglino and Jean-Louis Cousin of Le Relais Occitan (http://perso.orange.fr/relais.occitan/index.htm) for their hospitality in the Languedoc.

Finally, I would like to thank my wife Jo for her editorial expertise and support.

Artist's note

Readers may care to note that the original paintings from which the colour plates in this book were prepared are available for private sale. All reproduction copyright whatsoever is retained by the Publishers. All enquiries should be addressed to:

Peter Dennis, Fieldhead, The Park, Mansfield, NOTTS NG18 2AT e-mail: magie.h@ntlworld.com

The Publishers regret that they can enter into no correspondence upon this matter.

The Fortress Study Group (FSG)

The object of the FSG is to advance the education of the public in the study of all aspects of fortifications and their armaments, especially works constructed to mount or resist artillery. The FSG holds an annual conference in September over a long weekend with visits and evening lectures, an annual tour abroad lasting about eight days, and an annual Members' Day.

The FSG journal *FORT* is published annually, and its newsletter *Casemate* is published three times a year. Membership is international. For further details, please contact:

The Secretary, c/o 6 Lanark Place, London W9 1BS, UK

Contents

Introduction

In the early 13th century, the north of what is now France went to war with the south in a bloody crusade that lasted for the best part of half a century. It pitted Christian against Christian in a bitter conflict that saw gross excesses on both sides.

The ostensible reason for the crusade was to exterminate a heretical sect known as the Cathars that had grown strong in the south and permeated every level of society. By the end of the conflict, what had been an independent area was subsumed under the royal authority of the Capetian kings of France, who vastly extended their direct authority over the area. A whole way of life had been destroyed, along with the prosperity of one of the richest regions of the country.

As was the case with most medieval conflicts, pitched battles were rare. The Albigensian Crusade, as it came to be known, was characterized by small-scale skirmishes, vicious guerrilla actions and the besieging of the innumerable fortified sites that dotted the landscape of the south during this period, from the extensive Gallo-Roman fortifications of the great centres such as Toulouse, Narbonne and Carcassonne, through to the isolated hilltop fortifications that proliferated in the countryside. All these defences needed to be reduced – many of them more than once – and the remains of many of them still exist to this day, known somewhat inaccurately as 'Cathar Castles'.

A brief history of the Languedoc

In the early 13th century the area of southern France known as the Languedoc stretched from the Rhone Valley in the east to the River Garonne in the west, and from the Auvergne in the north down to where the modern region of Roussillon begins in the south. This area had a cultural unity that distinguished it from the north of France – it had different systems of land ownership and inheritance and even spoke a different language, the *langue d'oc* or *Occitan*.

The Romans had occupied the region following their victory over the Carthaginians in the Second Punic War and founded the city of Narbo (modern-day Narbonne). By 70 BC the whole area south of Lyon and Toulouse was known as Narbonensian Gaul. Further conquests by Julius Caesar and his imperial successors pacified the rest of Gaul and the Languedoc became an imperial province in 27 BC, with Narbonne as its capital.

By the 5th century AD the impact of waves of migrant Germanic tribes began to be felt in the area. First the Vandals passed through, then the Suevi and finally the Visigoths, who established a kingdom in the area based on the city of Tolosa (Toulouse). Initially the Roman authorities authorized this kingdom and the Visigothic king ruled as an imperial governor; however, the region rapidly became independent of any Roman authority.

In the late 5th and early 6th centuries AD the area was attacked by yet another wave of Germanic invaders, the Franks under their king Clovis. He defeated the Visigothic king Alaric II in AD 507 and absorbed much of his kingdom, including Toulouse itself, though some areas remained independent, such as Carcassonne. Further invasions came from the south in the 8th century AD, as Arab Muslim forces destroyed the Visigothic kingdoms both in Spain and across the Pyrenees. The Frankish leader Charles Martel turned the Muslim conquest back at the battle of Poitiers in AD 732 and the region was gradually reconquered by the Franks, first under Pepin the Short and then, decisively, under his more illustrious son Charlemagne. The region was split between the kingdoms of Aquitaine, Septimania (so named after the seven cities of Narbonne, Agde,

Béziers, Maguelone, Lodève, Nimes and Uzès) and the Spanish March, later to become the county of Barcelona. In order to rule his vast empire, Charlemagne instituted the comtal system – with appointed officials, counts and viscounts, possessing land and honours in return for undertaking governmental and defensive duties. With Charlemagne's death central authority over the counts grew weaker, and areas on the fringes – such as the county of Barcelona – rapidly became independent, whilst the appointed officials began to treat their offices as hereditary possessions, creating a new territorial aristocracy.

The lords of the south

These independent lords became the new masters of the south, creating a patchwork of territories with complicated ties of allegiance. As a result, no single central power could dominate the whole of the Languedoc.

The most important single lord in the region was the count of Toulouse, a hereditary honour held by the St Gilles family. Descended from Fredelon, appointed by Charles the Bald in AD 849, the family – named after the town from which they ruled their domains – grew in power throughout the 10th and 11th centuries through a series of prudent marriage alliances until they directly controlled large areas of the Languedoc. In the late 11th century Raymond IV of St Gilles became one of the leaders of the First Crusade, dying in the County of Tripoli in 1105.

The greatest rival of the house of Toulouse for control of the Languedoc was the house of Barcelona, which acquired the kingship of Aragon in 1137 through marriage. These two great houses fought for power throughout the 12th century and the lesser noble families – the counts of Foix, and viscounts of Béziers, Carcassonne, Narbonne and Montpellier – sought to exploit the conflict by transferring their allegiances from one lord to another to obtain the maximum independence for themselves. In 1150 the Trencavel viscount of Béziers and Carcassonne did homage to the king of Aragon for his territory, as did the count of Foix the following year. By the time peace was confirmed by the Treaty of Perpignan in 1198 the house of Toulouse was forced to concede that it had lost control of a substantial part of its territories – particularly the Trencavel lands, the county of Foix and the viscounties of Narbonne and Béziers. These lands passed into the realm of influence of the kings of Aragon and were the reason

The silhouette of the fortress of Quéribus stands out against the skyline, revealing clearly the three different levels of fortification. Although Quéribus was largely rebuilt following the end of the Albigensian Crusade remnants remain of the original fortification dating from the time of the Cathars. (Author's collection)

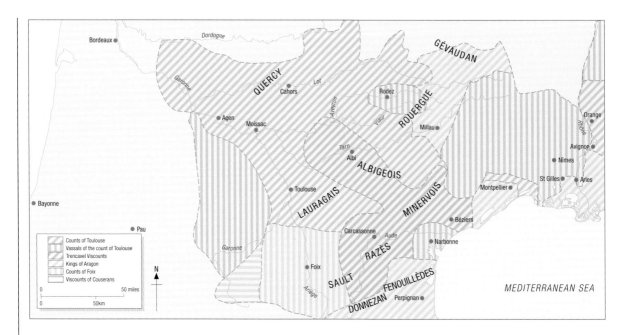

The following labels appear on the map:

Bordeaux • | Dordogne | GÉVAUDAN
Garonne | QUERCY | Lot | Rodez • | ROUERGUE | Orange •
• Agen | Cahors | Aveyron | Vibur | Millau • | Rhône
Moissac • | Tarn | Albi • | ALBIGEOIS | MINERVOIS | Avignon •
• Bayonne | • Toulouse | LAURAGAIS | Montpellier • | St Gilles • | Arles •
• Pau | Garonne | Carcassonne • | Aude | • Béziers
Counts of Toulouse | RAZÈS | • Narbonne
Vassals of the count of Toulouse | • Foix | SAULT | FENOUILLÈDES
Trencavel Viscounts | N | Ariège | DONNEZAN | Perpignan • | MEDITERRANEAN SEA
Kings of Aragon
Counts of Foix
Viscounts of Couserans
0 — 50 miles
0 — 50km

This map illustrates the divided loyalties that stretched across the Languedoc. Although the count of Toulouse, together with his vassals, controlled the lion's share of the region, the Trencavel possessions and other counties and viscounties that owed allegiance to the royal house of Aragon divided his lands. This lack of political unity was to prove a severe problem for the southern lords with the coming of the Albigensian Crusade in 1209.

for Pedro of Aragon's involvement in the events of the crusade in the 13th century. Although under the suzerainty of the kings of Aragon, these counties and viscounties had great autonomy and so the Languedoc, riven by conflict throughout the 12th century, entered the 13th facing a new threat – one which its lords were unable or unwilling to join together to defeat.

The Cathar heresy

This fragmented region proved to be an ideal breeding ground for the heresy known to history as Catharism. The 12th century was a time of religious upheaval throughout Western Europe: the Gregorian reforms of the late 11th century had renewed the Catholic Church's sense of moral and spiritual purpose, but they had also encouraged a wealth of popular response, not all of which was wholly orthodox.

Charismatic preachers, such as Peter of Bruis and Henry of Lausanne, travelled throughout the south preaching anticlerical messages, burning crucifixes and condemning the riches and excesses of the established church. Further north in the region around Cologne an organized heretical group was discovered in 1143. In 1145 St Bernard of Clairvaux went on a preaching tour of the Languedoc, ostensibly to counter the teachings of Henry of Lausanne, and he discovered an undercurrent of unorthodoxy that caused him to sound the alarm.

The heretics discovered both around Cologne and in the Languedoc were dualists. They believed that there were two equally powerful deities – one good, one evil. The 'good' god, whom they associated with the god of the New Testament, was master of the spiritual world and the human soul. The material world, and all things in it, was the realm of the 'evil' god, associated with the god of the Old Testament. The body was therefore a material trap for the soul, and life was to be spent in penance in order that the soul should not be reincarnated into the material world, which was considered a living hell.

The most devout amongst the dualists therefore rejected sex and parenthood as this equated to bringing another poor soul into the world of torment. They also refrained from eating any meat or other animal products, as they were created through reproduction.

These kinds of beliefs had existed since before the foundation of the Christian Church in the religion of Zoroastrianism, and there is an intellectual tradition linking the Cathars to the Gnostics and Manicheans of the early

Christian Church, who applied elements of the dualist Zoroastrian teachings to the Christian message. Evidence as to how these beliefs were transmitted to Western Europe is somewhat sketchy, but there is enough material to suggest that the Bogomils, a dualist sect originating in what is now Bulgaria, played a significant role in bringing the dualist doctrine westwards.

In contrast with the teachings of the traditional Christian Church, the Cathars rejected all of the Old Testament, apart from the Ten Commandments. They did accept large parts of the New Testament – though they denied the humanity, death and resurrection of Jesus Christ – which led to them rejecting all forms of violence and oath taking – and considered themselves to be 'good Christians'. They wholeheartedly rejected all the sacraments and symbols of the Catholic faith, rejecting the established Church as the 'harlot of the apocalypse' and 'church of wolves'.

The Cathars in the Languedoc became much more visible in 1165 when a debate was organized between representatives of the heretics and a number of Catholic bishops, abbots and the viscount of Béziers-Carcassonne. The heretics were condemned but allowed to leave unharmed.

This two-part early 14th-century image comes from the *Chronique de France ou de Saint Denis*. The left-hand portion depicts Pope Innocent III (1160–1216), who called for the Albigensian Crusade in 1208, excommunicating the heretics. The right-hand illustration depicts the outcome, as mounted knights cut them down. (Permission British Library, Royal 16 G.VI f.374v)

The Languedoc is home to many different sorts of fortification, from the imposing walls of Carcassonne to the remote hilltop castles of the Fenouillèdes. Among the more unusual types are the *circulades*, fortified villages arranged in a circle around a prominent feature, often the local church. This aerial shot depicts the village of Bram. (Service communication-CdC Piège Lauragais)

In 1167 a more significant council took place at Saint-Félix-Lauragais near Castelnaudary. Attended by many of the leading Cathar figures from the Languedoc, the council was addressed by one Nicetas, an eastern dualist who had travelled from Constantinople via Lombardy. This meeting formalized the Cathar doctrine and organized the heretical church in the region. From this point on the Languedoc was split into bishoprics, with each bishop having two successors beneath him, a *filius major* (elder son) and a *filius minor* (younger son). With the death of the bishop the *filius major* would take his place whilst the *filius minor* would become the *filius major*, with someone else taking up the junior role.

The men who filled these roles were *perfecti* or the Perfect, the most senior of two different levels of the Cathar faith. They had committed themselves to a life of poverty, celibacy and strict abstinence from eating meat. They had undergone a ceremony known as the *consolamentum* to become confirmed in their status, and any breach of their rigorous code of discipline would mean that their status as one of the Perfect would be lost and they would have to start the process all over again. The majority of Cathars belonged to the lower level of the sect – the *credentes*, or believers. They were not subject to the same restrictions as the Perfect, but were expected to bear witness to the faith and possibly take the *consolamentum* on their deathbed. From this point on Catharism became an organized church in the Languedoc and as such, posed a direct threat to the established Catholic hierarchy.

The Catholic Church's response

Following St Bernard of Clairvaux's preaching mission in 1145, the Catholic Church realized that it had a problem on its hands and sought to address the issue. At the Council of Tours in 1163 Pope Alexander III condemned the heresy in the Toulousain and Gascony, describing it as 'a cancer'. In 1168 Count Raymond V of Toulouse sent a letter pleading for help to clear his lands of heretics. The response was the despatch of a mission of high-ranking clergy led by the Papal legate in France, Peter of Pavia, and the abbot of Clairvaux, Henry of Marcy. This mission investigated heretics in the Toulousain and found a number of offenders. The next measure taken by the Church was a decree at the Third Lateran Council of 1179, threatening force against the heretics. The years following the death of Pope Alexander III saw little action against the heretics and enabled them to strengthen the structure of their newly organized church. There were a number of reasons for this inactivity on the part of the authorities: the fact that there were five short papacies prior to the accession of Innocent III in 1198; the battle of Hattin in 1187 that severely weakened the power of the crusader states in the east; and the ineffectual nature of the local ecclesiastical authorities in the south. However, in 1198 Pope Innocent III was elected; he was determined to root out heresy throughout the church so that he could unite Christendom behind a crusade to reverse the losses suffered by the crusader states. He started off by sending legates on a preaching tour throughout the Languedoc and Barcelona. These men were to have the power to excommunicate heretics; whilst in 1200 he passed the decree *Vergentis in senium*, which called for the property of heretics to be confiscated. He also appointed further legates – Peter of Castelnau in 1203 and Arnold Amaury, abbot of Clairvaux, in 1204.

These legates were joined at Montpellier in 1206 by the Spanish Bishop Diego of Osma and his assistant Domingo de Gúzman, better known as St Dominic. The two Spaniards persuaded the papal legates that the way to impress the Cathars was to act as their Perfect did, renouncing worldly wealth and travelling around preaching whilst living a life of apostolic poverty. They proceeded to travel around the Languedoc preaching, entering into debates with the Cathars, and attempting to persuade them of the errors of their ways.

At the same time that Innocent promoted preaching missions to attempt to convert the Cathars, he used political means to rid the area of heretics. He put pressure on Count Raymond VI of Toulouse to suppress the Cathars in his lands, and wrote to Philip-Augustus, king of France, promising him a crusading indulgence if he would go south to crush the heretics. Matters came to a head in 1207 when Peter of Castelnau excommunicated Raymond VI because of his lack of cooperation with the Catholic authorities. Following a visit to the count's court at St Gilles around Christmas 1207, no accommodation was possible between the two parties and Peter of Castelnau left in January 1208. On 15 January he was waylaid as his party stopped by the Rhône; a knight struck him down with a lance, killing him. When he heard that his personal representative in the Languedoc had been cut down, apparently on the orders of Raymond VI, Innocent III re-emphasized Raymond VI's excommunication and launched the Albigensian Crusade against the Languedoc, offering crusading indulgences, as well as the property of the heretics, for all those who took part.

The scene was set for the invasion of the Languedoc by northern French nobles and their men, all actively supported by the Catholic Church.

The fortifications of Carcassonne are some of the most striking examples of medieval defensive architecture in Europe. Lavishly restored by Eugène Viollet-le-Duc in the second half of the 19th century they have been included on the UNESCO World Heritage List since 1997. (Courtesy of Nikolai Bogdanovic)

Chronology

Design and development

Gallo-Roman sites

Many of the most important sites in the region were founded prior to the Roman occupation of the Languedoc in the 1st century BC. The Celtic tribes that occupied the region created hill forts – *oppida* – on the higher ground, and sites such as Carcassonne gained their first fortifications in this period. The major towns and cities of the region such as Béziers, Carcassonne, Narbonne and Toulouse were all important centres during the era of Roman occupation, and from the late 3rd and early 4th centuries AD they acquired the defensive walls that characterized their fortifications through to the medieval period. These walls were solidly constructed and studded with towers, and were reinforced and maintained through the Visigothic, Islamic and Frankish occupations. The major urban development of the 10th and 11th centuries was the addition of exterior settlements to these fortifications – the *bourgs*. Narbonne had a *bourg* by AD 978, Toulouse by 1078 and Carcassonne and Béziers certainly possessed them by the end of the 11th century. These suburbs to the Gallo-Roman centres were in turn fortified with walls and ditches, though not to the same extent as the older parts of the towns, and they were often the weak links in the defensive circuits – and the first attacked by the northern crusaders following their invasion in 1209.

Away from the large centres, there is evidence of Celtic and Roman involvement in some of the smaller fortifications. Archaeological work at Quéribus and Peyrepertuse has found Celtic remains, whilst Roman coins have been found on the site of Montségur. However, it is not until the 10th and 11th centuries that these smaller fortified sites, so characteristic of the Languedoc during the era of the Albigenisan Crusade, start to proliferate.

The medieval *castra*

By the end of the 9th century AD the Languedoc had suffered wave after wave of incursions and invasions. Visigoths, Muslims and then Franks had fought

This semicircular tower in the walls of Carcassonne has all the hallmarks of the original Gallo-Roman fortifications of the city. Its shape is characteristic of the defences of the late Empire, updated over time to form part of the medieval fortifications. (Author's collection)

The *castrum* of Fanjeaux provides another example of a fortified village of the Cathar period. Fanjeaux was the location of a debate between the Cathars and Domingo de Gúzman, better known as St Dominic, in 1206. Domingo later settled here and founded a nunnery for converted Cathar women in the valley below. (Service communication-CdC Piège Lauragais)

over large swathes of the region, whilst in the 9th and 10th centuries there were Norman and Magyar raids. This endemic warfare drove the local populace to seek shelter within protected settlements, known as *castra*.

The Latin word *castrum* (pl. *-a*) has a number of different meanings when it comes to fortifications. It can refer to freestanding fortifications, but more often it refers to the entirety of a fortified site, which may contain a central defensive element that corresponds to what modern readers might consider a castle. The chronicler Peter of les Vaux-de-Cernay in his history of the Albigenisan Crusade refers to the *castrum* of Cabaret, but also to the *munitio* of the *castrum* of Cabaret; *munitio* is perhaps best translated as 'castle'. This implies that the medieval notion of *castrum* is more closely linked to a fortified village than freestanding castle.

These *castra* start to appear throughout the Languedoc from the end of the 10th century; one of the first mentions of them occurs in a bull of Pope John XV, where he refers to a *castellum* belonging to the Abbey of Cuxa in the Fenouillèdes,

The *castrum* of Alairac was originally defended by an 11th-century fortification based on an earlier Visgothic site; this was taken and destroyed by Simon de Montfort in April 1210 as he sought to consolidate his hold on the area. The tight network of streets around the village church would have all been incorporated into the defences. (Author's collection)

This view of the castles of modern-day Lastours is taken from the principal fortification of Cabaret and shows (from front to rear) Tour Régine, Surdespine and Quertinheux. The defences visible in this photo largely postdate the events of the Albigensian Crusade, particularly in the case of Tour Régine, which was built *c.*1260. (Author's collection)

which has been tentatively identified with Puilaurens. This fortification certainly existed by 1011 and other fortresses appear in records of the early 11th century, notably in the will of Bernard Taillefer, Count of Bésalù, which records the first mentions of the fortifications of Peyrepertuse, Quéribus and Aguilar.

Throughout the 11th and 12th centuries these small-scale fortifications proliferated throughout the region; this process was closely linked to the rise of the *milites*, a military aristocracy based on the land who rose to power thanks to grants from the various counts and viscounts throughout the region, often on land taken from the great abbeys such as Lagrasse. The 12th century saw endemic fighting in the Languedoc between the powerful magnates of the region – the counts of Toulouse, Barcelona and Foix, Trencavel viscounts of Béziers and Carcassonne, and others – as each sought to maximize his own territorial control at the expense of his neighbour. These great magnates granted estates to their vassals, creating a lower level of aristocracy, which in turn created the numerous *castra*.

The castle of Puivert dominates the village of the same name that nestles beneath it. Simon de Montfort took the site in 1210 following the fall of Termes. The castle was extended during the 14th century, but a substantial part of the 13th-century fortification survives to this day. (Author's collection)

The abbey of Lagrasse, in the upper right of this picture, was one of the most important religious foundations of the region. Founded in AD 788, by the mid-12th century it controlled over 100 churches, as well as many secular estates. (Courtesy of Nikolai Bogdanovic)

These *castra* are many and varied in shape and size, but tend to belong to a number of recognizable styles. The most defensively secure are those perched in isolated positions on rocky precipices, such as Peyrepertuse and Quéribus. Others were less isolated, but still situated on heights above the surrounding countryside, such as Termes and Aguilar. Others took advantage of the landscape to protect themselves on one or more sides with precipitous drops, like Minerve, Padern and Quillan. *Castra* can also be found situated on the plains in amongst the fields, though these types of fortifications are rarer than the others; Arques and Villerouge-Termenès are two good examples.

One of the main problems with having so many of these fortifications based on hilltops and rocky platforms was the lack of nearby water supplies. Although they would all have possessed cisterns to store rainwater, very few of them had any immediate access to a supply of running water. It is a problem that crops up continuously throughout the narratives of the crusade; many of the sites were forced to surrender through lack of water.

When it comes to the construction of the *castra* themselves, the choice of style depended upon the location, as this tended to define the shape of the settlement and hence the defences. The principal fortification of these sites would have consisted of a simple tower keep (*castellum*), often protected by a thick wall, with a ditch running around it. These simple fortifications did not have chapels attached as the village church served both purposes. One of the defensive peculiarities of the Languedoc is the number of circular villages (*circulades*) where the streets are constructed in a concentric ring running out from a central point, often the village church or a *castellum*. Bram and Alairac are both good examples of this type of *castrum* that some claim owes its origin to a purpose-built programme of construction by Count Bernard Aton of Carcassonne in the mid 12th century.

This image depicts the gate-tower of the castle of Quillan, which was owned by the archbishop of Narbonne. Taken by Simon de Montfort in 1210 it was restored to the archbishopric prior to 1232, when it was extensively redeveloped. (Author's collection)

The royal fortifications of the Languedoc

With the fall of the Languedoc to the northern crusaders in the 50 years following the start of the Albigensian Crusade a new style of fortification became commonplace in the region: the French royal fortress.

These fortifications were designed in particular to protect the southern border of newly acquired French territory, something increasingly important following the Treaty of Corbeil in 1258. This treaty between Louis IX of France and James I of Aragon fixed the border between the two kingdoms in return for the French crown renouncing any claims they might have to territory in Catalonia, whilst the king of Aragon renounced any claims of overlordship to territory in the Languedoc and Provence. This left the new frontier running along the northern boundary of the modern region of Roussillon.

The imposing central keep of Peyrepertuse dominates the lower enceinte of the castle. It consists of two separate structures – a church and living quarters – joined by thick, crenellated walls creating an interior courtyard. (Author's collection)

The fortifications of the Fenouillèdes, which had held out against the northern invaders, now formed bastions along their southern frontier and were fortified as such. Peyrepertuse, Quéribus, Termes, Aguilar and Puilaurens became known as the 'five sons of Carcassonne', which itself was reinforced with another line of walls to become the citadel of the Languedoc.

Characteristic features of this new wave of fortification include the near-total destruction of the medieval *castra* at these sites, and the relocation of their populations to positions nearby. These fortifications were to be isolated from the populations they controlled. The royal defences were also constructed on a much greater scale than the *castra*, often possessing multiple enceintes with towers protecting the walls. The number of buildings inside the walls multiplied, providing accommodation and stores for the garrisons that now occupied the sites. They acquired chapels specifically to serve the fortresses. These fortifications were updated throughout the centuries to reflect the increasing role of gunpowder within siege warfare, and remained active until the mid 17th century.

This square tower is part of the castle of Foix on the edge of the Pyrenees, seat of the counts of Foix. The castle was extensively redeveloped throughout the 14th and 15th centuries, but this, the northernmost of three towers, contains the oldest elements, dating from the 12th century. (Author's collection)

Tour of the sites

Carcassonne

History

The site now occupied by the city of Carcassonne has been lived on since the prehistoric period, and there was certainly a fortified settlement, 2km south of the present-day *Cité*, from the 8th century BC onwards; archaeological finds of Etruscan and Greek pottery indicate that it was a trading post.

It was occupied during the Celtic period by a tribe called the Volcae Tectosages who fortified it as an *oppidum* (hill fort), and it was at this point that the site gained the name 'Carsac'. Following the Roman occupation of the area in the 1st century BC the hilltop was fortified again and became the *colonia* of Julia Carsaco, later Carcaso.

During the late Roman Empire period, the increased threat from Germanic incursions and political instability led to the fortification of Carcaso (or Carcasona) around the end of the 3rd century AD.

From the 5th century AD the city became part of the Visigothic kingdom of Toulouse, and remained part of the kingdom after the defeat of the Visigothic king Alaric II by the Merovingian king of the Franks, Clovis, in AD 507 and the capture of Toulouse. The city was besieged by the Franks the following year and formed part of the frontier between the two Germanic kingdoms.

Following the Arab invasion of the Iberian Peninsula, the Visigothic kingdoms were destroyed and in AD 725 Muslim forces captured the city. This was to prove a short-lived occupation as the Franks under Pepin the Short retook the city in AD 759, and it became part of the Carolingian Empire under Pepin's son Charlemagne. It was Charlemagne who introduced the comtal system to this part of the world, though the title of count was never intended to become a hereditary honour; rather it was to be an appointment governed by the Frankish monarchy. With the gradual erosion of central authority that followed the death of Charlemagne, however, these posts became directly inherited and were guarded within the important families of the region.

The counts of Carcassonne were members of the same family as the counts of Barcelona, one of the most important lords of the region, and by 1120 Bernard Aton, viscount of Béziers, had obtained the title by marriage into the family, thus joining the two honours. Bernard's great-grandson, Raymond-Roger, perished in the dungeon of the *Cité* in 1209 and his title, along with possession of the city, passed into the hands of Simon de Montfort. Following Montfort's death outside Toulouse in 1218 his son Amaury inherited his title, only to renounce it in favour of the crown in 1224. From this date onwards, Carcassonne became a royal possession – governed in the king's name by a series of seneschals.

NEXT PAGE **Carcassonne**
This is a representation of Carcassonne as it might have looked immediately prior to the siege by the crusaders in 1209. A single curtain wall, studded with towers, protects the city, whilst there are two suburbs, the St Michel and the Castellar, outside the main city walls. Inside the city itself stands the comtal castle (**1**), constructed from 1120, and basilica of St Nazaire (**2**), built in the Romanesque style. An inset (top right) shows the fortifications following their reconstruction in the late 13th century. The *bourgs* have been destroyed, with the population moved to the other side of the Aude, and a second ring of defences has been placed around the city. Inside the walls the cathedral of St Nazaire has received some gothic additions whilst the comtal castle has been rebuilt and been given a defensive wall facing towards the town.

During times of conflict it was customary to augment the permanent masonry defences with wooden hoardings projecting beyond the walls. These enabled defenders to cover the bottom of the walls and prevent the besiegers from getting close enough to undermine them. These reconstructions are found on the walls of the comtal castle at Carcassonne. (Author's collection)

The fortifications

The earliest fortifications of Bronze Age Carcassonne consisted of a simple ditch with a raised rampart inside it. This basic system of defence – ramparts, ditches, protected gateways – no doubt prevailed throughout the Celtic and early Roman occupation and it was not until the late empire, when central control broke down and instability was rife, that Carcassonne acquired the system of walls that define it today.

This initial circuit consisted of a strong masonry wall, enclosing an area of 7 hectares, which was studded with between 34 and 40 towers situated between 18 and 35m apart. These towers were c.14m high and semi-circular. The bottom floor was usually solid to prevent undermining, whilst the upper level had openings to either side allowing access to the walkway along the top of the wall. In common with many other Gallo-Roman towns of the period there were probably four major entrances to the town. The exact date of the construction of these early fortifications is unknown, but they were certainly in place by AD 333, as by this point Carcassonne had received the designation *castellum* and formed one of the stopping points on the pilgrimage route from Bordeaux to Jerusalem.

This Gallo-Roman structure formed the basis for the fortifications of Carcassonne throughout the medieval period, though they were extensively rebuilt under the Visigoths during the 5th and 6th centuries AD. Following the Carolingian occupation of the area in the 8th century AD the town became the possession of counts, finally ending up in the hands of the Trencavel family. Bernard Aton, the first count of this line, reorganized the defences of the *Cité*. He invested a number of knights with responsibility for individual towers in the city walls – for which they were to receive a house within the *Cité* and lands outside the walls. He is also believed to have constructed the comtal palace, which was built from 1120 onwards.

There had been subsidiary settlements outside of the walls of the *Cité* itself (*bourgs*) since the Gallo-Roman era, and by the time of the crusade there were three of these: the St Vincent near the banks of the River Aude, which was unguarded; the St Michel to the north of the *Cité*; and the Castellar to the south. The latter two were both protected with walls and ditches.

By the time of the crusade the defences were much as they had been in the mid 12th century, with the only additions being wooden hoardings added immediately prior to the approach of the crusaders. These projected out beyond the walls, covering the ground at their base to prevent sappers from approaching close enough to undermine the structures.

Following the fall of Carcassonne in 1209 Simon de Montfort occupied the city and, while he kept the defences in a state of readiness, there is no evidence that they were improved or changed to any great extent. It was only when Carcassonne became a royal possession after 1226 that changes started to occur, with the development of an outer line of fortifications to reinforce the existing walls. In 1240 Raymond-Roger Trencavel besieged the city, and once again the defenders used wooden hoardings to extend the defensive power of the walls. Nevertheless, Trencavel came very close to reconquering his family's ancestral seat, not least because of the help he received from the inhabitants of the *bourgs*. Following the eventual failure of his siege and the suppression of the more general rebellion, the defences of Carcassonne were redoubled.

Firstly, the *bourgs*, which had provided so much support for the Trencavel force in 1240, were razed to the ground and their population transported to a newly built suburb on the other side of the River Aude – the bastide St Louis. The second line of walls was developed whilst the inner walls were largely torn down (particularly where they had been damaged during the siege) and replaced. The new defences generally followed the line of the original enceinte, though there was a considerable extension to the south of the *Cité*. Also, the new towers were quite different in their design: they were round (with the exception of the Bishop's Tower and the gate tower of St Nazaire, which were square), did not have a solid lower floor, and also generally consisted of four or five different floors. The comtal palace was also reinforced, particularly on the side facing the *Cité* where it gained a semicircular barbican. This extensive reconstruction work took place during the reigns of Philip III and Philip IV, stretching into the early 14th century.

Peyrepertuse

History

Although archaeologists have found evidence that the site of the fortress at Peyrepertuse had been occupied since the 1st century BC, and the territory called the *pagus Petra Pertusense* is mentioned as being part of the county of Razès from the 9th century AD onwards, it is not until the 11th century that a fortification is first recorded there. This first mention occurs in the will of Bernard Taillefer, the count of Bésalù, dating from 1020. Mentions of the fortress are rare over the next 150 years, but it is clear that the site, along with the region of the Pérapertusès associated with it, became part of the lands of the count of Barcelona in 1111, before being handed over to his vassal the viscount of Narbonne in 1112, along with the fortifications of the Fenouillèdes, in return for assurances of his support.

As part of the domains of the viscount of Narbonne, Peyrepertuse played no part in the opening years of the Albigensian Crusade. It is only when the viscount of Narbonne's overlord, Pedro of Aragon, aligned himself with the counts of Toulouse and Foix in hostilities against Simon de Montfort, culminating in the battle of Muret in 1213, that this area of the Languedoc was drawn into the conflict.

Following his victory at Muret, Montfort claimed the titles of count of Toulouse and duke of Narbonne, with the viscount paying homage to him. In 1217, William of Peyrepertuse followed his overlord in acknowledging Montfort's mastery. However, by 1226 his fortress had been confiscated and granted to Nunyo Sanche, count of Roussillon, a vassal of Louis VIII and, later,

When approaching the hilltop fortress of Peyrepertuse, the first sight of the defences is the imposing northern wall overlooking the gorge. This 120m-long wall is over 1.2m thick and has two towers. At the near end is a triangular-shaped bastion while the entrance to the castle is located at the far end. (Author's collection)

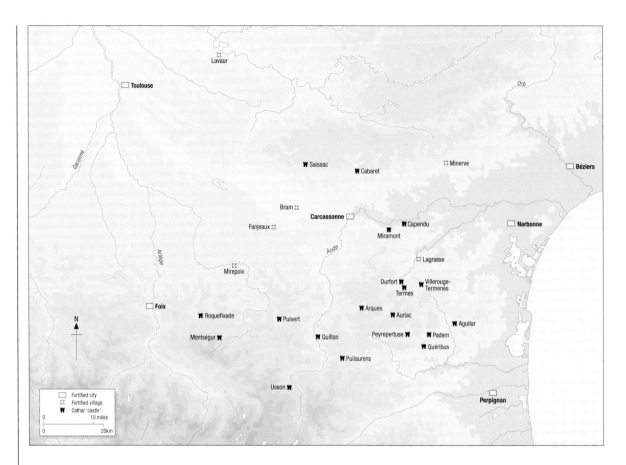

This map highlights the principal fortified cities, villages, and castles within the Languedoc.

Louis IX. Sanche sold the castle directly to Louis IX in 1239. The following year it appears that William of Peyrepertuse occupied his old lands once more during the revolt of the *faidits* – the dispossessed southern lords. Jean de Beaumont, chamberlain of Louis IX, besieged Peyrepertuse and, on 16 November 1240, William of Peyrepertuse surrendered to the forces of the crown.

From this point onwards the castle remained firmly in French royal hands and, following the Treaty of Corbeil of 11 May 1258, Peyrepertuse stood on the front line between the kingdoms of France and Aragon-Castille – one of the 'five sons of Carcassonne' protecting the south from foreign invasion.

The fortifications

The fortress of Peyrepertuse is situated 800m above sea level on a rocky platform. The site consists of three separate sections: the lower enceinte, the middle enceinte, and the higher fortification of San Jordi.

It is difficult to state with any great certainty which, if any, of the fortifications that cover this rocky platform existed under the stewardship of William of Peyrepertuse prior to the occupation by royal forces. It is probable that the *castrum* of the Cathar period consisted only of elements of the central keep and the church of St Mary, surrounded by the dwelling places of the inhabitants.

OPPOSITE **Peyrepertuse**
The fortress of Peyrepertuse became one of the most imposing defences along the southern border of France following its refortification in the second half of the 13th century. Here it is shown following these improvements, with a 120m-long curtain wall on the northern side containing the main entrance (**1**), protected by a barbican (**2**). The internal buildings consist of the keep complex (**3**), which housed the church of St Mary (**4**) and the commander of the castle's quarters (**5**), and a further domestic structure along the south wall (**6**). At the very tip of the fortress was a triangular-shaped bastion (**7**, shown in the inset) that dominated the valley below.

Following the royal occupation in 1240, Peyrepertuse was the only fortification in the region directly controlled by the crown – nearby Quéribus was still controlled by *faidit* lords. An intensive programme of fortification followed William of Peyrepertuse's surrender and, in the years 1250/51 over 100 men were at work refortifying the site. It was during this period, and later in the 13th century, that the fortifications that now dominate the site were erected.

The lower enceinte is triangular shaped and protected on its northern side by a 120m-long wall, 1.2m thick, with two semicircular towers projecting over the gorge below. The main entrance to the fortress is situated at the near end of this wall, protected by an exterior barbican covered by arrow slits in the main wall. At the far end of this wall stands a triangular-shaped bastion, consisting of three levels equipped with numerous arrow slits. The southern wall runs along the edge of a precipitous drop over which the fortresses latrines are situated. This wall would also have had a tower on it, though little of this remains. Further along stands the remains of a two-storey stone-built building, which may well have held water cisterns. Beyond this lies the keep of the fortification.

The keep consists of two main structures – one building consisting of living quarters and store rooms, the other housing the church of St Mary along with a water cistern. The two buildings are joined by thick walls to create a single structure with an open courtyard in between. There are two gateways to the keep: one opens onto the interior of the lower enceinte, the other leads outside the walls of the enceinte to the next level of fortifications.

The middle enceinte leads to the steps of St Louis, which in turn lead up to the fortification of San Jordi. This higher fortification, constructed during the great building project of 1250/51, contains a further chapel, two water cisterns, living quarters and towers over the lower and middle enceintes.

Quéribus

History

The history of Quéribus is very similar to that of Peyrepertuse – throughout the 11th and 12th centuries generally the same lords controlled them. The first mention of this site also occurs in the will of Bernard Taillefer, count of Bésalù, in 1020, where it is referred to as *Popia Cherbucio*. The subsequent ownership of the site followed the same pattern as that of Peyrepertuse, falling under the sway of the counts of Barcelona and becoming part of the territory of the viscount of Narbonne. It is only with the coming of the Albigensian Crusade that differences start to appear.

The walls of the town of Lagrasse provide a good example of a medieval system of integrated defence, with the houses backing onto the River Orbieu forming an exterior wall that protects the site. (Author's collection)

Quéribus did not become part of the crown possessions like Peyrepertuse and was still an active haven for Cathars in the mid-13th century – in 1241 Benoît of Termes, the Cathar deacon of Razès, died there. Its lord during this period was the redoubtable Chabert of Barbera, who continued to hold out against the encroaching royal fortresses until he was captured and imprisoned in the castle of Aguilar by his erstwhile ally Olivier of Termes. With his departure Quéribus proved vulnerable and was captured by royal forces under Pierre of Auteuil, seneschal of Carcassonne, in 1255.

Following its capture Quéribus was refortified in the late 13th century to suit its new position as part of the first line of French defences along the southern border.

The fortifications

The fortress itself stands at a height of 728m guarding the pass of the Grau de Maury. It consists of three different terraced levels perched on the mountain top, built in a mixture of styles from the 11th century and updated up until the 16th century. The top level contains the castle keep – this dominant polygonal structure towers over the fortifications below and was constructed during the 13th century after the royal occupation. It probably replaced an earlier 11th-century structure, as some of the lower masonry dates from that period. The walls of this keep are some 3–4m thick. The interior of the building consists of a 7m-high split-level chamber with a vaulted ceiling, joined to a tower in which a spiral staircase accesses the roof.

The keep opens onto a courtyard, within which are located a number of smaller structures, including a water cistern. This courtyard is surrounded by a wall. Descending from the upper level of fortifications, the second level contains a further water cistern and barracks for the defenders, pierced with loopholes overlooking the valley below and the path up from the lower level of the fortifications.

The lowest level of the fortifications contains the entrance to the site, defended by loopholed walls and an arched passageway.

Cabaret (Lastours)

History

The *castrum* of Cabaret gave its name to the area of the Montagne Noire known as the Cabardès. The area is first mentioned in documents around 1063 and the site was held under the authority of the viscount of Béziers and Carcassonne.

At the time of the crusade Peter-Roger was lord of Cabaret and he served his lord, Raymond-Roger Trencavel, at the siege of Carcassonne (see pages 40–42). Following the fall of the city, Peter-Roger escaped back to Cabaret and it formed a centre for resistance to Montfort's rule in the area. The chronicler Peter of les Vaux-de-Cernay refers to it as 'outstanding in its opposition to Christianity and the Count, a veritable fountain of heresy'. Montfort attempted to besiege the site at the beginning of the campaigning season of 1209, but failed in his endeavour – despatching the mutilated defenders of Bram to the site in 1210 as a grisly warning of his intent. In the end Cabaret fell to the crusaders through negotiation in 1211 following the fall of Lavaur. Peter-Roger made his peace with Montfort and withdrew; the castle was then occupied by one of Montfort's lieutenants, Bouchard de Marly, who had actually been imprisoned in the castle for the previous 16 months.

Following the death of Montfort outside the walls of Toulouse in 1218 Cabaret once more became a haven for Cathars until it finally passed into royal hands following the Treaty of Paris in 1229.

The remains of the castle of Cabaret, one of the four fortifications of Lastours. The castle consists of a five-sided keep (visible in the foreground) attached to living quarters and surrounded by a curtain wall. This divides the interior of the castle into two sections, at the back of which stands a tower. (Author's collection)

The oldest settlement at Lastours was the medieval *castrum* of Cabaret. Over the last 20 years this area has been uncovered by archaeological work, which has revealed that it was constructed during the 12th century and abandoned after the crusade, possibly having been destroyed by royal forces. The *castrum* is located just below where the four castles stand, down by the River Grésillou. (Author's collection)

The fortifications

Although four separate fortifications now stand on the site, only three of them were present during the period of the crusade – Cabaret, Surdespine and Quertinheux. The fourth, Tour Régine, was built following the royal occupation of the site, probably around 1260.

The medieval *castrum* of Cabaret was located beneath these four fortifications, lower down the slope by the banks of the River Grésillou. This medieval site was constructed some time in the late 11th and early 12th centuries and consisted of a basic fortification, around 500m^2, located on a ridge with a simple keep and a rectangular building attached to it. On either side of this fortification the streets of the medieval *castrum* led down to the rivers Grésillou and Orbiel.

The four fortifications higher up the slopes of the hill were all heavily reconstructed following the royal occupation and share similar characteristics. The fortress of Cabaret consists of three principal elements: a five-sided keep with slits for archers and a large window looking west: a rectangular stone building used for living quarters and a stout curtain wall protecting them both. The curtain wall had a walkway along it and a tower at the northern end. A barbican protected the gate.

The next castle in line, Tour Régine, was originally called Tour Neuve, reflecting its later development. It consists of a tall tower surrounded by a wall. The tower itself has certain similarities with the towers constructed in the walls of Carcassonne during the same period. It is accessed by means of an external ladder going up to the first floor and has mounts for the attaching of wooden hoards around the upper levels.

Surdespine consists of a rectangular tower and a lower stone building, between which is located a water cistern. The whole complex is surrounded by a stone wall, within which there were originally other buildings, but no trace remains of these.

The final fortification, Quertinheux, consists of a tower constructed at the same time and to the same design as that of Tour Régine, surrounded by a complex curtain wall that divides the interior into a number of different courts. These contain two water cisterns; the entrance was protected by a projecting wall, which created a kind of chicane.

The four fortifications of Lastours stand on rocky outcrops high above the village of the same name. They are (from left to right) Cabaret, Tour Régine, Surdespine and Quertinheux. Only three were present at the time of the crusade; royal forces constructed Tour Régine following their occupation of the site. (Author's collection)

Peyrepertuse keep

Following the royal occupation of the castle of Peyrepertuse the keep was extensively rebuilt to provide accommodation and storage facilities, as well as protection for the garrison. Following the archaeological work of Lucien Bayrou, this illustration is a tentative reconstruction of how the interior might have looked towards the end of the 13th century. The right-hand building houses the church of St Mary as well as an extensive water cistern to the rear; the left-hand building houses the garrison commander's quarters as well as store rooms. Walls link both buildings to create a single defensive unit. In the years 1258 to 1260 the garrison of Peyrepertuse consisted of nine sergeants-at-arms, one chaplain and the commander of the castle, one Gaufred de Malbois.

The fortress of Montségur sits on top of its *pog* (Occitan for 'hill') dominating the surrounding countryside. This view is from the south-west, the direction from which the royal forces tried to attack in 1243/44, without much success. (Author's collection)

Montségur

History

Much of the history of Montségur comes to us through the Inquisition record of Raymond of Pereille, who was lord of the place. In 1204 he was asked by senior Cathars to fortify the site to act as a refuge for members of the sect. It was certainly known to the Catholic authorities, for at the Fourth Lateran Council in 1215 Bishop Fulk of Marseille accused Count Raymond-Roger of Foix of allowing the fortified Cathar site to remain in territory of which he was overlord. In 1232 Guilhabert of Castres, the Cathar bishop of Carcassonne, was resident there. It was he who asked Raymond of Pereille to allow the Cathar community who had gathered there to live within the walls of the fortification, and the site acted as a centre for the Cathar Perfect who were being hunted across the Languedoc. By 1233 the site was being referred to by Catholic clergy as the 'Synagogue of Satan'.

The royal seneschal of Carcassonne, Hugh of Arcis, finally besieged the site in April 1243 and, after an 11-month siege it fell to the royal forces in March 1244 (see pages 50–53). Following its capture the site was handed over to Guy of Lévis II, who did homage to Louis IX for it in July 1245; from this point on it became a bastion on the Franco-Spanish border and no longer a haven for heretics.

The fortifications

Montségur stands on a 1,200m-high hill (or *pog* in Occitan) and there are three distinct phases in the development of its occupation and fortification: the initial defences that stood prior to the redevelopment by Raymond of Pereille after 1204, known as Montségur I; the *castrum* constructed by Raymond of Pereille and conquered by royal forces in 1244, known as Montségur II; and the royal fortification built by Guy of Lévis II some time after 1245, known as Montségur III.

Of Montségur I practically nothing is known. Archaeological finds point to the fact that there was a settlement here, but the scale and extent of it are unknown.

Montségur II, the *castrum* of the Cathars, is better preserved, though the central area lies underneath Guy of Lévis' fortification. What survives on the central part

This view of one of the streets of Bram around the church strikingly shows the curvature of the *circulades*. Bram was the site of one of the first massacres of the crusade, when Montfort mutilated the defenders before driving them out and sending them to the Cathar stronghold of Cabaret. (Author's collection)

At the end of the 9th century AD Charles the Simple gave the territory of Padern to the Abbey of Lagrasse, and a fortification is recorded here from the early 11th century onwards. The castle was largely rebuilt by the Vic family in the 16th century and finally abandoned around the end of the 18th century. (Author's collection)

of the hill are three levels of terraces on the northern side, clustered around the base of the later fortifications. There are also terraces to the west of the summit to the rear of Montségur III. These terraces held numerous small houses and would have formed the living quarters for the majority of the Cathar population of the site during the siege. At the centre of the summit, directly beneath Montségur III, it is reasonable to assume that there was some sort of a central fortification. This probably took the form of a primitive keep with living quarters attached, similar to that found at the medieval *castrum* of Cabaret. To the south-west, the natural approach to Montségur, there was a series of defensive walls descending the steep slope and a barbican. About 100m to the east stood another barbican, followed by a series of three defensive walls. Further east, past the 'Avenue des Trebuchets', at the north-east point of the hill, stands the Roc de la Tour, and there was a further defensive feature situated here – described as a tower by the chronicler William of Puylaurens – below which an 80m sheer cliff falls away.

These fortifications were levelled following the royal occupation of the site and the village of Montségur was moved to the base of the hill, where it stands today. Where the Cathar *castrum* once stood a royal fortress was erected and it is the remains of this fortification that are now visible on the site.

This imposing fortress consists of two main sections: a square keep and a courtyard surrounded by a curtain wall mounted by a wall walk. Along most of its length the curtain wall is 1.5–2m thick; however, the far wall, facing the direction from which the crusaders attacked, is almost double the thickness. The interior of the courtyard is empty, but would certainly have contained wooden structures for the housing of the garrison, for use as storerooms and for sundry other purposes. The keep of Montségur is joined directly to the curtain wall and consists of two levels. The access to the keep is via a wooden ladder to the first floor, which could be removed if the courtyard fell. There is also an arrow slit facing into the courtyard, emphasizing that the keep was designed to be held on its own if necessary. There is also a water cistern on the ground floor.

Other sites of interest

Aguilar

The castle of Aguilar was certainly in existence by 1020 and had been granted by the Trencavel counts to the Termes family by 1084. Following the capture of Raymond of Termes after the fall of his castle of the same name, Aguilar became a possession of Simon de Montfort who granted it to Alain of Roucy. Olivier of Termes regained the castle during the revolt of the *faidits* in 1240, only to lose it again shortly afterwards. Following his reconciliation with the French crown it was restored to him in 1250 and he sold it to Louis IX in 1260 when it became a royal fortification – one of the 'five sons of Carcassonne', protecting the southern approaches to the city.

Quéribus

This view from below shows the castle of Foix towering over the buildings of the town. The circular tower to the front is a later addition, but the two square towers behind would both have been present at the beginning of the 13th century, albeit in a different form. (Author's collection)

The fortifications of Aguilar are split between those constructed by the Termes family in the late 12th century and the royal defences built after 1260. They consist of a central keep surrounded by a five-sided curtain wall. Outside of this stands a further six-sided curtain wall with a semicircular tower at each corner. A semicircular bastion protects the gate.

Arques

The castle of Arques stands on the plain about 1,500m west of the village of Arques. In 1125 Count Bernard Aton of Carcassonne granted the fortification to the Termes family. Following the disenfranchisement of the family by Simon de Montfort the fortification passed into the hands of the crusaders and, by 1231, it was owned by Peter of Voisins. The castle that stands today was constructed between 1280 and 1316 and consists of a 24m-high keep with towers on each corner, all surrounded by a 55 × 51m curtain wall with a central gate.

Foix

The castle of Foix was the seat of the counts of Foix, one of the most powerful noble families of the region. The house of Foix was founded at the beginning of the 11th century when Count Roger of Carcassonne divided his lands and gave the territory around Foix to his youngest son Bernard-Roger. The castle dates from this period. During the Albigensian Crusade Count Raymond-Roger of Foix (d.1223) was one of the most vehement opponents of the crusaders – perhaps unsurprisingly, as his sister Esclarmonde was a Cathar Perfect.

During the course of the crusade the castle was besieged unsuccessfully in 1212, but was nevertheless handed over to the papal legate in 1214 and Raymond-Roger was only able to return following the death of Simon de Montfort in 1218. After the Treaty of Paris French royal troops occupied the castle for five years before it was handed back to Roger-Bernard of Foix, Raymond-Roger's son.

OPPOSITE **Quéribus**
The castle at Quéribus was extensively rebuilt after it fell into royal hands after 1255; this reconstruction shows it in the late 13th century once the work had been carried out. The defences were based on three separate levels, with a polygonal keep dominating the top level of fortifications. The pathway up to this central fortification is protected by two lower stages, each of which covers the progress towards the centre of the castle. The upper right inset shows the entrance to the highest level of Quéribus.

The castle of Aguilar sits on a hill rising above the plain of Tuchan. It formed part of the territory of the lords of Termes and, following their defeat by Simon de Montfort in 1210, was occupied by the crusaders before finally being restored to Olivier of Termes in 1260. (Author's collection)

The castle as it stands today consists of two square towers, linked together, along with a large circular tower, all of which are surrounded by a curtain wall. The circular tower was constructed after the period in question, being built at the beginning of the 15th century.

Minerve

The town of Minerve, centre of the Minervois region, is situated at the confluence of the rivers Brian and Cesse. Originally a possession of the counts of Carcassonne, it came under the suzerainty of the king of Aragon from 1179.

Under its lord William of Minerve the town provided a sanctuary for Cathar Perfect during the early years of the crusade. This sanctuary was destroyed when Simon de Montfort laid siege to the place in 1210, capturing it within two months.

Little now remains of the castle that protected the landward side of Minerve. The principal defensive feature of the town was its naturally strong location, perched high above the two rivers.

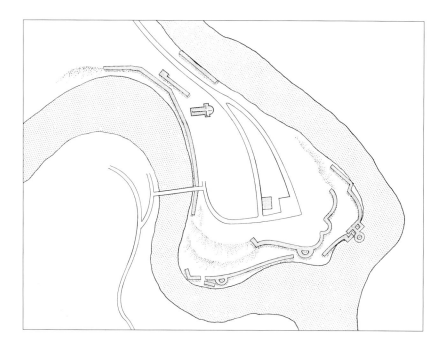

The fortified town of Minerve was situated on a rocky promontory between the rivers Brian and Cesse. A strong castle protected its landward side during the period of the Albigensian Crusade. Its only weaknesses were that the land on the opposite banks of the river was the same height, making it vulnerable to siege weapons, and that its water supply was located at the bottom of the gorge. (Artwork by John Richards, copyright Osprey Publishing Ltd)

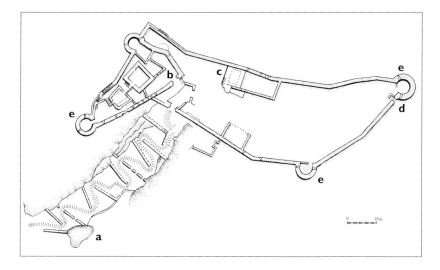

This plan of Puilaurens (after Quehen and Roquebert) shows the complicated entrance to the castle (a); the path upwards is broken by a series of later walls that would have slowed any potential attacker. This dated from the beginning of the 16th century. Inside the main enceinte we find many of the standard features: a central keep (b), water cisterns (c), posterns (d), and towers (e). (Artwork by John Richards, copyright Osprey Publishing Ltd)

Puilaurens

The castle of Puilaurens formed part of the viscounty of Fonollède, in the county of Bésalù. It was one of the last of the fortifications of the region to fall into royal hands; the Cathar deacon Peter Paraire is recorded as staying here in 1241 and it became a refuge for Cathar Perfect following the fall of Montségur in 1244. However, by 1258 it was certainly in royal hands as, following the Treaty of Corbeil, Louis IX sent instructions to the seneschal of Carcassonne to refortify the site and it became one of the 'five sons of Carcassonne'.

The oldest part of the fortifications is the square keep at the centre of the site, dating originally from the 11th century. In the 12th century this building was enlarged and surrounded with a curtain wall. Following the royal occupation the site was enlarged and towers were built at the angles of the enceinte.

The distinctive entrance to the castle, via a path blocked by successive walls that create a kind of defensive chicane, was not built until the beginning of the 16th century.

Puivert

Puivert was built from 1152 by Bernard of Congost, who obtained the land from the viscount of Carcassonne. During the Albigensian Crusade the castle was taken

The castle of Puilaurens was one of the last of the Cathar strongholds to fall to the French crown. In 1241 Pierre Paraire, the Cathar deacon of the Fenouillèdes, stayed here and it provided a refuge for some Cathars following the fall of Montségur in 1244. By 1258 it was in royal hands and was refortified to act as one of the border defences of the French kingdom. (Author's collection)

The four fortifications of Lastours – Cabaret (**1**), Tour Régine (**2**), Surdespine (**3**) and Quertinheux (**4**) – dominate the skyline overlooking the River Orbieu. They are shown here as they would have appeared towards the end of the 13th century following their occupation and reconstruction by northern French forces. Of the four, three predated the Albigensian Crusade, whilst Tour Régine was constructed around 1260.

Archaeological work in recent years has shown that the medieval *castrum* of Cabaret was located to the left of the main image, situated on a series of terraces leading down to the river and dominated by a primitive stone keep. The inset image recreates what some of this medieval habitat may have looked like.

The imposing gate-tower and front wall of Puivert was constructed around 1310 by Thomas of Bruyères, the descendant of one of Simon de Montfort's lieutenants. The original castle from the Cathar period is located to the rear of the structure. (Author's collection)

by one of Simon de Montfort's lieutenants, Thomas Pons of Bruyères-le-Châtel, in 1210 following a three-day siege. The Congost family was disinherited and Bernard of Congost, lord of the family, died in Montségur in 1232 having received the *consolamentum*; his sister had already died a good Cathar death in 1208. Bernard's son Gaillard was one of those involved in the massacre of Catholic inquisitors at Avignonet in 1242, whilst his sisters died in the massacre following the fall of Montségur in 1244.

The castle was developed in two main periods. The old castle was constructed in the 12th century and consists of small enceinte with a keep near the entrance. In the 13th and 14th centuries the castle was enclosed within a considerably larger curtain wall. In the middle of one of the shorter sides of the wall stands a square gate-tower while there is a further square tower in the south wall and a round tower in the north wall. Directly opposite the entrance, against the far wall, stands a three-storey, 35m-high keep, which served as the living quarters for the lord of the place.

Termes

The castle of Termes was the seat of the family of the same name, which possessed a number of castles throughout the area known as the Termenès. This family was closely linked with Catharism and the brother of the lord of Termes at the time of the crusade became a Cathar bishop responsible for a considerable portion of the Aude valley, whilst the chronicler Peter of les Vaux-de-Cernay describes Raymond of Termes as 'a manifest heretic who feared not god nor regarded man'. During the Albigensian Crusade Simon de Montfort took Termes after a four-month siege (see pages 44–45) and it remained in crusader hands until it was recaptured by Olivier of Termes during the revolt of the *faidits* in 1240. Olivier did not hold onto his castle for long and it was in royal hands by

Cabaret (Lastours)

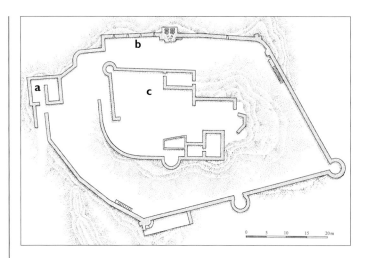

1250, being refortified and becoming one of the 'five sons of Carcassonne'.

The castle itself stands at a height of 500m overlooking the village of the same name. It was probably built in the early 12th century but extensively modified once it became a royal possession in the mid-13th century. The fortifications consist of a double enceinte. The exterior wall, 8–10m high, is pierced with arrow slits and the entrance lies in the south-east corner, protected by a watch-tower. The inner wall is very badly damaged – the castle was blown up in the mid-17th century to prevent bandits using it – but it is possible to make out the locations of a keep, chapel and water cisterns.

The castle of Termes gave its name to the region of Termenès and was one of the most important fortifications of the area. In this plan (after Quehen and Roquebert) the entrance to the castle can be seen protected by a dogleg turn (a). Other defensive features include a number of machicolations (b). The keep is long destroyed but was probably located in the centre of the fortifications (c). (Artwork by John Richards, copyright Osprey Publishing Ltd)

Toulouse

Although nominally ruled by the house of Toulouse, the inhabitants of the city of Toulouse had gained a great deal of autonomy for themselves during the course of the 12th century. The fact that the counts of Toulouse generally lived in St Gilles on the other side of their lands ensured that they were unable to exercise direct control over the city and by 1152 a council was running most of the affairs of the town, whilst in the 1170s the leaders of the city were calling themselves consuls (*capitouls*) in a conscious imitation of the town's classical past. Although prior to the crusade the townspeople had often been in conflict with their counts, for its duration they supported him and held out against sieges in 1211 and, most famously, 1217/18 (see pages 48–50).

Little survives today of the medieval fortifications of Toulouse; the only buildings from the period that have stood the test of time, though altered, are the great churches, such as the Basilica St Sernin. The original defences of the city were Gallo-Roman in origin, and consisted of a 2.5m-thick, 5m-high wall that featured towers every 35–40m. This fortification only covered the area known as the *Cité* and in the 12th century a further wall, studded with towers, was built around the *bourg* of St Sernin that had grown up by the side of the old town. Across the River Garonne stood a further *bourg*, St Cyprien, but this was unfortified.

Unlike Carcassonne, very few of the medieval fortifications of Toulouse have survived. Like many of the Gallo-Roman towns and cities of the region Toulouse consisted of a number of areas. The oldest, and best defended, section was the *Cité*, whilst a wall also protected the Bourg St Sernin. Across the Garonne, the suburb of St Cyprien was unprotected. Despite its name, the Saracen Wall is not in fact an Islamic structure. (Artwork by John Richards, copyright Osprey Publishing Ltd)

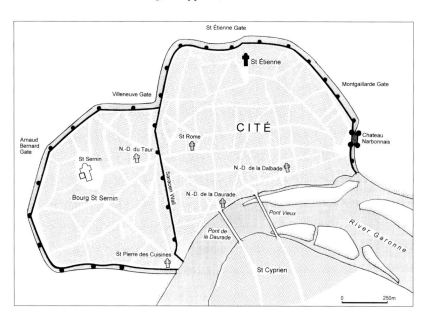

Faidit lords and crusader knights

Prior to the northern intervention in the Languedoc, southern feudal society was quite distinct from its northern counterpart. In the north feudalism was a much more rigid concept. Great magnates controlled large areas of land, which they then granted to lesser nobles in return for oaths of loyalty and ties of vassalage. These lesser nobles were then compelled by these ties to serve their masters, fighting for them if necessary. The whole structure was legitimized by the church and the code of chivalry that begins to appear in the late 12th century.

In the south matters were arranged rather differently. The great magnates of the south, such as the count of Toulouse and the viscounts of Béziers and Carcassonne, were never able to impose the same ties of vassalage on the lesser nobility that developed in the Languedoc. Instead, the lesser nobility managed to maintain their own independence to a large extent, entering into deals with the large landowners into return for land (*conventiae*) but never being tied into the close bonds of obedience that characterized the relationships that existed amongst their northern counterparts. The location of their remote strongholds in the hills of the Languedoc also served to bolster their independence, and the chronicler Peter of les Vaux-de-Cernay states of Raymond of Termes that 'so confident was he in the strength of his *castrum* that from time to time he was prepared to take up arms against the king of Aragon, the count of Toulouse or his overlord the viscount of Béziers'. Even in the dark days of the Albigensian Crusade, when Simon de Montfort was conquering the southern strongholds one by one, these fiercely independent lords were unwilling to give up their rights. Three of the more powerful lords, Peter-Roger of Cabaret, Aimery of Montréal and Raymond of Termes, sought the protection of Pedro of Aragon, offering to acknowledge him as their overlord. However, they baulked at his insistence that he be granted control over their *castra* and the deal was never concluded.

Another great difference between the southern lords and the northerners was the system of inheritance. In the north primogeniture – the inheritance of the estate by the first-born child – was the practice. In the south the influence of Roman law and custom still held sway and inheritances could be divided according to the will of the possessor of the property – a concept known in the south as *paratge*. In practice this could lead to a large number of multiple seigneuries, with many lords having a share of the same area. Some of the larger landowners of the region, the counts of Toulouse and the lords of Termes among them, used the system of primogeniture to ensure the cohesion of their estates, but over time this concept of *paratge* changed to simply reflect the southern way of life as distinct from the northern invaders.

Indeed, by the end of the 12th century a distinct southern courtly life had developed, promulgated by the troubadours. Although the sophistication of this culture has been overplayed by modern enthusiasts who seek to depict pre-crusade Languedoc as a medieval utopia, there is some truth to the argument that as the Languedoc contained a larger number of independent noblemen, so it fostered a large number of independent courts – each seeking to outdo the other with the sophistication of their displays. The troubadour tradition thrived in this environment, and the travelling musicians could be sure of a welcome in the remote hilltop fortifications of the Cabardès and the Fenouillèdes.

It was in this distinct southern culture, with its powerful, lesser nobility that Catharism flourished, protected by these selfsame nobles. The chronicler William of Puylaurens recounts how when Bishop Fulk of Toulouse reproached a Catholic knight for not prosecuting heretics, the knight replied that he could not, as he

The abbey at Lagrasse was one of the major landowners in the region and controlled a large number of the hilltop fortifications such as Padern and Arques. (Author's collection)

had been reared in their midst and had relatives living amongst them. This certainly seems to have been the experience of the southern nobility. There is no evidence to accuse Count Raymond-Roger of Foix of being a Cathar, yet it is clear that his sister Esclarmonde was a Cathar Perfect and it appears that his wife, Philippa, ran a house for female Cathar Perfect.

The coming of the northern crusaders changed this world completely. When Simon de Montfort assumed the title of viscount of Béziers and Carcassonne, he rapidly began to dispossess the lords in the Trencavel territories who would not submit to him, removing their inheritance and turning them into what became known as *faidits* – dispossessed knights who fought for the southern cause. In their place Simon appointed his own lieutenants, men such as Bouchard of Marly and Guy of Lévis, to create a new aristocracy in the region.

In 1212, following Raymond VI of Toulouse's excommunication, Simon de Montfort called a *parlement* at Pamiers and announced a series of statutes for the way the south was to be run. Apart from many features concerning dues to the church and the treatment of heretics, what stands out is Simon's desire for control through vassalage over all the land that he gave to his supporters; no one was to build fortifications without his consent. He also declared that from this point onwards the northern rules of inheritance would apply and that any southern heiress of a fortified site was to be married to a northern nobleman. The southern aristocratic way of life changed forever.

The sites at war

From 1209, when the crusaders first entered the Languedoc, until the fall of Montségur in 1244 warfare was endemic throughout the region. Pitched battles were few and far between, though the battle of Muret on 12 September 1213 proved to be particularly decisive; moreover, the conflict comprised a fight for control of the many fortified sites throughout the region. The summer campaigning season would see the northern French attempt to reduce the various southern strongholds before most of the crusaders returned to their homes following the 40-day stint required of them in order to gain a crusader's indulgence.

Once the bulk of the army had withdrawn the crusader garrisons were left isolated and open to attack by the southern lords, who sought to regain their territory. It is this ebb and flow of conquest and reconquest focussed on isolated hilltop fortifications, small towns and fortified villages that characterizes the Albigensian Crusade and its aftermath. The following examples highlight some of the major actions that define the period.

Béziers, 1209

On 9 October 1208 Pope Innocent III issued a Bull urging people to take the cross against the heretics of the Languedoc, offering them all the benefits that the status of crusaders allowed – remission of sins, cancellation of all debts to Jews and those to fellow Christians suspended, and their property to be protected by the papacy whilst they were on the crusade. Responsibility for preaching the crusade was given to the head of the Cistercian order of monks, the abbot of Cîteaux Arnold Amaury, who was also to lead the crusade.

Although Philip-Augustus, king of France, did not become personally involved in the crusade he permitted some of his major magnates to go and such notable northern French nobles as the duke of Burgundy and count of Nevers joined the expedition, as well as others who were to become famous, such as the count of Montfort. The host gathered at Lyons towards the end of June and, on 2 July, they were joined by Raymond VI, the count of Toulouse, who had reconciled himself with the church in an effort to protect his lands in the south.

The crusaders carried on down the Rhône Valley, resupplying at Nîmes and pausing at Montpellier where they were met by the viscount of Béziers and Carcassonne, Raymond-Roger Trencavel, who also sought an agreement with the crusaders in order to protect his lands from imminent invasion. Arnold Amaury rejected his approaches and the scene was set for the first armed confrontation of the crusade.

Raymond-Roger turned back towards the fortified city of Béziers and, deciding it was indefensible in the face of such a large opposing force, summoned his vassals to join him at Carcassonne where he withdrew together with the Jewish population of Béziers. The rest of the population of Béziers stayed to await the crusaders' arrival.

This illustration from *The Chronicles of France from Priam King of Troy until the Crowning of Charles VI* depicts the expulsion of Cathars from the city of Carcassonne. Of particular interest are the wooden additions to the defences of the walls, used to cover the base of the fortifications and prevent undermining. (Permission British Library, Cotton Nero E. II pt. 2)

The crusader army arrived outside Béziers and set up their camp to the south-west of the city. By 22 July 1209 they were in place, the encampments had been established, and they were ready for what could have turned out to be a long siege. The defences of Béziers were substantial, based on the Gallo-Roman walls and fortified throughout the medieval period. The inhabitants had also stockpiled plenty of supplies and one might suspect that they were confident that they could hold out until the crusader host broke up through lack of supplies, disease or simply due to the fact that the 40-day quarantine period for crusaders elapsed and they dispersed.

Some of the camp followers attached to the crusading army – the so-called *ribauds* – drifted close to the entrance of the citadel and provoked a sally by some of the defenders, who caught one of the camp followers, killed him and threw him into the River Orb. This in turn caused an all-out attack on the now-open gate by the camp followers and they forced their way through as well as scaling the walls with ladders. To this point the main bulk of the crusaders' army, the men-at-arms and knights, had not been involved in the attack but, when they saw what had happened, they surged forward to break into the defenceless town.

It is at this stage that one of the first of the many controversial episodes of the Abigensian Crusade is reputed to have taken place. According to a later chronicler, when asked by the soldiers how they were to distinguish between honest Catholics and heretical Cathars, Arnold Amaury responded: '*caedite eos. Novit enim dominus qui sunt eius*' – 'Kill them all. The Lord knows who are his own.' Whatever the truth of the matter, this is exactly what happened to the citizens of Béziers as described by William of Tudela in his history of the crusade:

And they killed everyone who fled into the church; no cross or altar or crucifix could save them. And these raving beggarly lads, they killed the clergy too, and the women and children. I doubt if one person came out alive ... such a slaughter has not been known or consented to, I think, since the time of the Saracens.[1]

Although the wholesale slaughter of towns that had resisted a siege was not unknown in the medieval period, the inclusion of women and children in the massacre was unusual and served as a foretaste of the atrocities that both sides would commit upon both combatant and non-combatant populations of the areas they conquered.

Following the slaughter, the *ribauds* set fire to the city, destroying many of the supplies and all of the plunder, and the whole of the army rested for three days before resuming their advance through the Languedoc. Between 15,000 and 20,000 people are estimated to have died in the slaughter.

Carcassone

The next target of the crusaders was the principal town of the Trencavel lands, the heavily fortified city of Carcassonne. En route to their destination the effect of the massacre at Béziers was immediately felt when the fortified city of Narbonne surrendered without any show of resistance and many of the lords of the various territories around Béziers and Narbonne sought to side with the crusaders. However, the taking of Carcassonne was to prove a tougher task.

Raymond-Roger Trencavel had gathered his vassals together and was determined to defend the town. He had also undertaken a scorched-earth policy outside the walls, stripping the countryside of anything that might prove useful to the crusaders. As described earlier (see pages 17–21) Carcassonne was strongly fortified. The medieval *Cité* stood on a rocky promontory defended by a stout enceinte of Gallo-Roman origin pierced by 26 towers. There were also two suburbs, the St Michel and the Castellar, that were less strongly defended.

---

[1] Shirley, Janet (tr.), *Song of the Cathar Wars: a history of the Albigensian Crusade by William of Tudela and an anonymous successor* (Ashgate Publishing: Aldershot, 2000) p. 21.

The second, outer layer of Carcassonne's defences was constructed following the failure of Raymond Trencavel to capture the town in 1240. The *bourgs* surrounding the walls were destroyed and the population moved to the far bank of the River Aude. A second enceinte was added surrounding the first, which was rebuilt, and the towers and gateways were strengthened. (Author's collection)

The crusading army started arriving around the city from 1 August 1209 and set up camp to the west of the fortifications, occupying the Pont Vieux across the River Aude and blocking access to the river from the city, thus leaving the inhabitants to rely upon the water supplies within the walls themselves. On 3 August the first assault came against the Bourg St Michel, the northerly suburb of the town. This suburb was only defended by a low wall with few towers and the crusaders managed to break through without too much difficulty, forcing the suburb's defenders back behind the walls of the *Cité*. Once they had occupied the *bourg* the crusaders demolished the fortifications and used the material to fill in the defensive ditches.

Whilst the crusaders were preparing to assault the stronger defences of the Castellar, Pedro, king of Aragon and Castile, intervened. As count of Barcelona he was the liege lord of Raymond-Roger Trencavel and he had no wish to see his vassal's lands taken from him. Pedro was a renowned Catholic prince, later to become famous for his victory against the Moors at the battle of Las Navas de la Tolosa in 1212, and the crusaders could not afford to ignore his request; he was allowed to go inside the *Cité* to consult with his vassal. Once inside King Pedro appears to have persuaded Raymond-Roger to seek terms; however, those offered by Arnold Amaury were totally unacceptable to the viscount and Pedro

The castle of Saissac is located to the north of Carcassonne in the Montagne Noire region. It appears in records from the late 10th century onwards and its lords were vassals of the Trencavel viscounts until they were dispossessed by Simon de Montfort and the castle passed into northern hands. The keep, square towers, and curtain walls visible here date from the late 13th to early 14th centuries. (Author's collection)

withdrew leaving the way clear for the siege to resume. On 7 August the crusaders started their assault on the second suburb, the Castellar, which they hoped would prove as open to direct assault as St Michel. However, the initial assault was forced back and the attackers were forced to resort to their siege machinery for the first time in the crusade. They first used what the chronicler Peter of les Vaux-de-Cernay refers to as 'petraries' to weaken the top of the wall before a wooden shelter covered with ox hides was forced against the foot of the wall in order to protect sappers who were to undermine the defences. Although the defenders managed to destroy this piece of siege machinery – called a 'cat' in other sources – the sappers had managed to gain a foothold at the base of the wall and, the following morning, the wall collapsed and the crusaders rushed forward to occupy the city. Once the suburb had been secured the bulk of the crusader army returned to their camp and it was at this point that Raymond-Roger made a sortie, massacring most of the garrison before he in turn was driven back by the returning crusader forces.

Following the fall of the suburbs, only the *Cité* was left in Trencavel hands and, by the middle of August, the situation was becoming desperate – shortages of water combined with the hot weather and the large number of people crammed into the *Cité* had led to outbreaks of disease. Raymond-Roger was invited to parley with the crusader leaders to discuss terms; he accepted the invitation and was quickly imprisoned once he had left the safety of the walls. Carcassonne was taken and the population were allowed to leave unharmed, though without any of their possessions. William of Tudela describes the scene as the inhabitants filed out:

> Out they came, citizens, knights, noblewomen and girls, each running as in a race until there was no one left in the town … Quite unprotected, they rushed out pell-mell in their shirts and breeches, nothing else, not even the value of a button were they allowed to take with them.[2]

Raymond-Roger was taken back into the *Cité* and imprisoned in his own comtal castle. He was to die three months later, ostensibly of dysentery.

Even before the death of Raymond-Roger the crusaders had decided to depose him and replace him with one of their own leaders. The title was offered to a number of the senior leaders of the crusade but they turned it down, and the title was offered to a lesser lord who had distinguished himself throughout the siege – Simon de Montfort. Although titular earl of Leicester, he was unable to claim his English lands due to Philip-Augustus' conflict with John of England, and only possessed a small estate near Paris. For this reason he was acceptable to Philip-Augustus, who had no wish to see one of his more powerful magnates acquire extensive estates in the south, and Simon became viscount of Béziers and Carcassonne. With this development, the bulk of the crusader army withdrew leaving Simon with around 500 men to protect his newly won domains.

Carcassonne was besieged once more in 1240, but this time it was a Trencavel assaulting the town. Raymond Trencavel, the disinherited son of Raymond-Roger, attempted to regain his inheritance through force and succeeded in taking the suburbs. However, the *Cité* held out, and Raymond Trencavel was forced to withdraw.

Minerve, 1210

With the fall of Carcassonne, the deposition of Raymond Trencavel and the accession of Simon de Montfort as viscount of Carcassonne and Béziers, many of the towns and strongholds of the Trencavel lands submitted themselves to their new lord. Towns such as Fanjeaux, Montréal, Castres and Limoux were handed over and garrisoned with northern soldiers. However, the countryside was by no

---

2 Shirley, Janet (tr.), *Song of the Cathar Wars: a history of the Albigensian Crusade by William of Tudela and an anonymous successor* (Ashgate Publishing: Aldershot, 2000) p. 26.

means pacified and with the bulk of the crusader army retiring northwards Simon de Montfort faced a struggle to hold onto his newly won lands. His first major setback was the failure to capture the triple fortress of Cabaret, located to the north of Carcassonne: its impenetrable location and the resilience of its lord, Peter-Roger of Cabaret, ensured that the northerners were forced to give up their attempted siege in September 1209. Other sites that had surrendered to him – such as Montréal and Castres – cast off their vows and went over to the other side, and lack of manpower forced Montfort to remain on the defensive. He lost over 40 castles according to the chronicler Peter of les Vaux-de-Cernay. However, the spring of 1210 brought further reinforcements from the north and he was able to attack once more.

One of the first targets of his new campaign was the fortified village of Bram. At the end of March Montfort besieged the town and, after three days, his forces broke through the defences and captured the village. Montfort was in no mood to be generous to the defenders and, according to Peter of les Vaux-de-Cernay:

> They put out the eyes of the defenders, over a hundred in number, and cut off their noses. One man was spared one eye so that, as a demonstration of our contempt for our enemies, he could lead the others to Cabaret.[3]

The chronicler excuses Simon for this atrocity by stating that the southerners had performed similar acts on captured crusaders, but it was clear that this conflict was to be extreme even by medieval standards.

Following his success at Bram, Simon moved on to the principal Cathar fortress near to his base at Carcassonne, Minerve. This fortified town, the centre of the Minervois region, occupies a very strong position with three sides protected by precipitous gorges, while a castle dominated the landward side. The site is described in the *Song of the Cathar Wars* as follows: 'There is no stronger fortress this side of the Spanish passes, except for Cabaret and Termes'. Its principal weakness, as with so many of the fortresses of the region, was its

This view of Minerve from across the River Cesse highlights the defensive strength of the position: the steep cliffs made it difficult to attack from two out of three sides. However, the town's water supply was located at the bottom of these cliffs, creating a weak spot here. (Author's collection)

[3] Sibley, W. A., and Sibly, M. D. (tr.) *The History of the Albigensian Crusade by Peter of les Vaux-de-Cernay* (The Boydell Press: Woodbridge, 1998) p. 79.

The imposing fortress of Termes, ruled by the family of the same name, dominated the area known as the Termenès. It held out against the crusaders under Simon de Montfort for over two months before a polluted water supply caused the defenders to abandon the site. (Author's collection)

water supply. The only access the population had to water in time of siege was through a protected passageway running to the bottom of the cliff. Montfort arrived at the site at the beginning of June and invested it from three sides. He set up three great siege engines – trebuchets designed to hurl large stones – to crush the protected passageway, one of which was nicknamed 'Malvoisine' ('Bad Neighbour'), and, according to Wiliam of Tudela:

> He laid siege to the place as he had planned, and set up his catapults, making Bad Neighbour the queen and lady of all his siege engines.[4]

The defenders, realizing that these weapons could cut off their water supply and render their position untenable, made a sortie in an effort to destroy them. However, this failed and by mid July the water supply had indeed been destroyed and the leaders of the resistance, under their lord William of Minerve, sought terms.

Given his treatment of the defenders of Bram, Montfort was surprisingly gracious, granting William a minor fief near Béziers in return for his lands around Minerve and permitting the population to go unharmed. However, there was a vital stipulation. The papal legate Arnold Amaury had arrived on the scene and he insisted that only those who reconciled themselves with the Catholic Church were to be allowed to go.

There was a substantial number of Cathar Perfects sheltered within the town and they were unwilling to give up their faith, replying to a Catholic bishop who tried to convert them, 'Why do you preach to us? We will have none of your faith.' Over 140 of them were taken out and burnt – the first mass burning of heretics of the crusade.

Termes, 1210

Following his success at Minerve, Montfort decided to tackle another of the great thorns in his side – the formidable hilltop fortress of Termes, situated to the south-east of Carcassonne.

---

[4] Shirley, Janet (tr.), *Song of the Cathar Wars: a history of the Albigensian Crusade by William of Tudela and an anonymous successor* (Ashgate Publishing: Aldershot, 2000) p. 33.

Termes was the centre of the region known as the Termenès and is described by Peter of les Vaux-de-Cernay as 'marvellously, indeed unbelievably, strong and in human estimation ... quite impregnable'.

Simon de Montfort's force arrived at the base of the fortress in August, having managed to weather a surprise assault on his siege train by the indefatigable Peter-Roger of Cabaret, who had made a sortie from his mountain refuge in an attempt to destroy the crusaders' siege machinery. The defenders of Cabaret continued to harass the crusaders throughout the siege of Termes, disrupting the flow of supplies and reinforcements to the besieging forces. The siege machines were a vital part of Simon's strategy for dealing with the hilltop fortifications of the Languedoc. Termes was no exception and he set up mangonels, trebuchets and *ballistae*, all of which were maintained with the aid of an archdeacon from Paris who organized a confraternity to both help pay for the siege engines and also to supply them with wood and stones. The expense of maintaining the besieging army was crippling and Simon is described as being so poor that he ran short of personal supplies.

The defence of Termes was organized by its lord, Raymond of Termes, who had fought against both the counts of Toulouse and viscounts of Béziers and Carcassonne, so was used to conflict. He was also reputed to be a Cathar. The defenders also made use of siege machines and came very close to hitting Simon de Montfort with a bolt from a *ballista* at one stage. They also made numerous sorties in an attempt to disrupt the crusaders and destroy their siege engines. One of Termes' few weaknesses was its water supply, and by mid October the levels in the cisterns had fallen dangerously low, leading the defenders to offer terms to Simon that gave him possession of the castle for the winter providing it was returned the following spring. These terms were accepted as Simon was not in a position of strength and unaware of the perilous state of the water supply inside the castle. However, the night before the handover was due to take place there was a sudden downpour that replenished the garrison's reserves. They refused to hand over the castle as agreed and the siege dragged on.

In November, following the arrival of reinforcements, the crusaders started to dig trenches close to the walls and the garrison, weakened through illness, decided to slip away by night. Their escape was discovered and Raymond of Termes was captured; he died three years later in the cells of Carcassonne. His son, Olivier of Termes, was to prove a constant enemy of the crusading forces until he was reconciled with the occupying forces in 1250.

One of the immediate effects of the fall of Termes was that Peter-Roger of Cabaret sought terms and handed over control of his fortress to Montfort in March 1211.

Lavaur, 1211

The year 1211 saw a number of important political developments in Montfort's struggle for control of the Trencavel lands. Firstly, Pedro of Aragon recognized Montfort's position as viscount of Béziers and Carcassonne, accepting him as a vassal. This was something he had been unwilling to do in 1209 immediately following the deposition and death of Raymond Trencavel, but he now realized that Montfort's position was so strong that he had to accept the inevitable. The second major development was the renewed excommunication of Raymond VI, count of Toulouse, by the papal legates in January, subsequently confirmed by the Pope in April. This meant that the count of Toulouse was no longer a crusader and his lands were no longer protected by the pope; in fact, as an excommunicate his lands were forfeit and there was an opportunity for Montfort and the northerners to entrench themselves in the south even further.

Following the submission of Cabaret the crusaders decided to advance on another town reputed as a haven for heretics, Lavaur, centre of the Lauragais region.

The siege of Toulouse 1217/18

46

Lavaur was held by the lady of the town, Geralda of Lavaur, supported by her brother, Aimery of Montréal, who had already been dispossessed of his lands by Montfort once before. The town was well defended, situated above the River Agout, with its cliffs protecting one side of the site, whilst the other sides were defended by thick walls – so thick that the defenders could ride their horses on them according to Peter of les Vaux-de-Cernay. Initially, the crusader forces were only strong enough to lay siege to one side of the place, but after reinforcements arrived they managed to construct a wooden bridge across the Agout and surround Lavaur.

Some of these reinforcements had come from an unusual source. The bishop of Toulouse, Fulk of Marseille, had organized a confraternity of loyal Catholics in the city – the White Brotherhood – who had otherwise been engaged in street fighting with their rivals, the Black Brotherhood, in the streets of Toulouse. At the end of March Fulk led his confraternity to take part in the siege, highlighting the divisions that existed within the south between the supporters of the old regime and the followers of the new lords.

Other reinforcements did not get to the siege. Towards the end of April Raymond-Roger, count of Foix, intercepted a column of German crusaders coming to reinforce Montfort's army and slaughtered them near the village of Montgey. William of Puylaurens claims 5,000 were killed, but the number is unlikely to have been so high. Montfort destroyed the village in May as revenge for this massacre.

Despite missing these reinforcements, Montfort's siege engineers carried on with the same work that they had undertaken at Minerve and Termes before, as Peter of les Vaux-de-Cernay describes in the passage overleaf.

Today little remains of the castle of Auriac, which was constructed in the early 11th century and belonged to the Termes family by 1173. It passed into northern hands during the Albigensian Crusade and was eventually abandoned during the 18th century. (Author's collection)

OPPOSITE **The siege of Toulouse 1217/18**

Although Simon de Montfort had slighted the fortifications of Toulouse in 1216, the city still managed to hold out against his forces from October 1217 to the beginning of July 1218. The inhabitants of Toulouse rallied behind their returned count, Raymond VI, and rebuilt the fortifications as best as they could, supplementing them with ditches and palisades to prevent the crusaders getting near the walls. When his direct assaults failed, Simon de Montfort ordered the construction of 'cats' (mobile shelters, shown here) to protect his troops so that they could get close to the walls to undermine the defences. It was whilst he was trying to protect one of these shelters from a sortie by the defenders of Toulouse that Montfort was killed on 25 June 1217. Simon is shown being hit in the head by a stone thrown by a mangonel (in the bottom left); his brother Guy has already been shot from his horse by a crossbowman and lies on the ground to Simon's right.

Whilst this was happening our men built a siege engine of the type commonly called a 'cat'. When it was ready they dragged it to the ditch surrounding Lavaur, then with a great effort they brought up wood and branches which they tied into bundles and threw into the ditch to fill it.[5]

Once the wall had been undermined and breached, the crusaders broke into the town on 3 May and captured it. Montfort was determined to make an example of the place for a number of reasons, including the fact that Aimery had submitted to him in 1210, the length of the siege, and the massacre of the German crusaders. What followed was a further example of Simon's ruthlessness and determination to put down any threat of revolt. He had Aimery of Montréal hanged along with 80 of his knights, against all the customs of medieval warfare. William of Tudela remarked that he had never heard of so great a lord being hanged in all of Christendom, and the weight of Aimery's armour broke the gallows. The Lady Geralda was also executed, as William of Tudela describes:

Lady Girauda was taken, and she shrieked, screamed and shouted. They held her across a well and dropped her into it, I know this for certain, and threw stones on top of her. This caused great dismay.[6]

A large number of Cathars, some 300 or so, were also burned on pyres outside the town.

Toulouse

As the most important city of the Languedoc, the centre of the Toulousain region and the base for the count of Toulouse, the city was an important prize for the northern crusaders. Raymond VI's reconciliation with the church in 1209 had ensured the safety of his lands but, following his further excommunication in January 1211, his possessions were now targeted. The principal problem for any army seeking to take Toulouse was its sheer size. This meant that a very large force was required to blockade the city and it is no wonder that many of the campaigning forces throughout the period sought to avoid a direct confrontation with the city, instead relying on pillaging the surrounding countryside and cutting Toulouse off from its sources of supplies and wealth.

The first siege of Toulouse was a somewhat desultory affair. Following his successful sack of Lavaur, Montfort turned his attention towards the city and approached it on 17 June. However, his forces were too small to cut the flow of supplies going into Toulouse and suffered continual harassment from those within the city, particularly Count Raymond-Roger of Foix. The siege was therefore lifted on 29 June, less than a fortnight after it had started.

In the end Montfort managed to obtain possession of Toulouse without bloodshed. Following his victory over Pedro of Aragon and the combined southern and Aragonese forces at the battle of Muret in 1213, he was the undisputed master of the Languedoc and spent the next few years consolidating his gains. Anxious to ensure that the extensive county of Toulouse should remain within his sphere of influence, Philip-Augustus of France despatched his son, Prince Louis, southwards with a substantial force to join the crusaders. Having suffered serious casualties at the battle of Muret and stripped of their political leaders, the great cities of the Languedoc were in no mood to resist the heir to the throne of France: first Narbonne submitted to the force and then, in May 1215, Toulouse also surrendered to the crusaders. Breaches were made in the walls, defensive ditches were filled, and the Chateau Narbonnais, fortress of the counts of Toulouse, was detached from the curtain wall to create an independent bastion

[5] Sibley, W. A., and Sibly, M. D. (tr.) *The History of the Albigensian Crusade by Peter of les Vaux-de-Cernay* (The Boydell Press: Woodbridge, 1998) p. 115.
[6] Shirley, Janet (tr.), *Song of the Cathar Wars: a history of the Albigensian Crusade by William of Tudela and an anonymous successor* (Ashgate Publishing: Aldershot, 2000) p. 42.

outside the city. Peter of les Vaux-de-Cernay states that 'the pride of the city of Toulouse was utterly humbled'. Prince Louis returned to Paris and the Fourth Lateran Council later in the year stripped Count Raymond VI of his land and titles, giving them instead to Montfort.

The lords of the Languedoc were unwilling to accept the papal judgment and the son of Raymond VI, also called Raymond, led a revolt in the south, occupying the town of Beaucaire in the winter of 1216. The following spring and summer Montfort besieged the southerners without success until August, when he learned of unrest in Toulouse and, fearing that he might lose his possessions, he returned to the city to pacify the inhabitants. This he did with some effect. He extorted large amounts of money from the citizens, took hostages, further levelled the fortifications and, finally, allowed his troops to sack the city. Having further alienated his new subjects, Montfort set off on additional campaigns in 1217, leaving his wife and family ensconced in the Chateau Narbonnais. In September Count Raymond VI slipped into the city to be greeted with a rapturous reception. The crusaders in the Chateau were isolated, those in the city itself killed, and the citizens of Toulouse sought to repair the damage done to their fortifications and await the inevitable response from Montfort. The *Song of the Cathar Wars* describes the process:

Men worked inside and outside the town fortifying its gateways and levels, its walls, bastions and double brattices, its ditches, lists, bridges and stairways.[7]

Simon de Montfort returned from his campaigns in Provence in October and immediately sought to break into the city through direct assault. However, the inhabitants had reinforced the defences sufficiently with ditches and other obstacles that the attackers could not break through and, by December, Simon realized that he would have to seek reinforcements. He sent his wife together with Bishop Fulk to Paris to preach the crusade and the following year reinforcements began to flood southwards. However, they still could not break down the defences through weight of numbers and Simon resorted once more to his siege machinery. Alongside the trebuchets and mangonels used to batter the walls, he decided to try undermining the fortifications and built more 'cats' to protect his sappers as they approached the walls, filling in the defensive ditches as they went. By 24 June these were ready and began to move forward towards the walls. Meanwhile, the defenders had also equipped themselves with similar weapons and managed to prevent the leading shelter from reaching the walls. Realizing that if these machines reached the defences their position would be seriously threatened, the defenders resolved to sortie from the walls in order to destroy them with fire.

Summoned from his prayers to help defeat this sortie, Montfort was struck by some sort of artillery projectile, as the *Song of the Cathar Wars* describes:

There was in the town a mangonel built by a carpenter and dragged with its platform from St Sernin. This was worked by noblewomen, little girls and men's wives, and now a stone arrived just where it was needed and struck Count Simon on his steel helmet, shattering his eyes, brains, back teeth, forehead and jaw. Bleeding and black, the count dropped dead on the ground.[8]

The seal of Raymond VII, count of Toulouse (1197–1249). Raymond inherited the county from his father, Raymond VI, in 1222 and struggled to keep hold of his birthright in the face of northern territorial ambition. He eventually came to an agreement with the French monarchy at the Treaty of Paris in 1229. (AKG-images/Erich Lessing)

[7] Shirley, Janet (tr.), *Song of the Cathar Wars: a history of the Albigensian Crusade by William of Tudela and an anonymous successor* (Ashgate Publishing: Aldershot, 2000) p. 141.
[8] Shirley, Janet (tr.), *Song of the Cathar Wars: a history of the Albigensian Crusade by William of Tudela and an anonymous successor* (Ashgate Publishing: Aldershot, 2000) p. 17.

OPPOSITE **The fall of Montségur, 1244**

The Cathar fortress of Montségur held out against the royal French troops under the seneschal of Carcassonne, Hugh of Arcis, from April 1243 until March 1244. This scene shows the final stages of the siege. The royal troops managed to scale the north-eastern side of the *pog* of Montségur and overpower the defences there; they then managed to lift siege machinery to the top of the hill and began to batter the inner defences of Montségur, which consisted of a series of defensive walls stretching down from a central site that probably contained a simple stone keep. The lower left inset shows the reconstructed fortress of Montségur, known as Montségur III, which was built by Guy of Lévis following the royal occupation of the site. This fortification was built on top of the Cathar fortifications and it is the remains of this site that can be seen today.

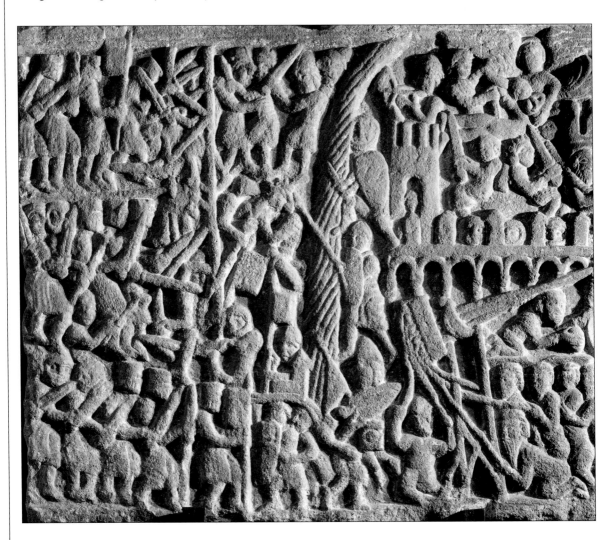

This 13th-century bas relief is located in the cathedral of St Nazaire in Carcassonne. It is believed to show the death of Simon de Montfort outside the walls of Toulouse in June 1218. Clearly visible in the bottom right-hand quarter of the relief is a representation of a mangonel, or stone-thrower – the cause of Simon's demise. (AKG-images/Erich Lessing)

With his death the siege, and the crusade in general, lost direction. His position was inherited by his son, Amaury de Montfort, who lacked the drive and determination of his father. The siege of Toulouse was lifted following one final attack on 1 July.

Another chronicler, William of Puylaurens, describes the devastating effect Simon's death had on the morale of the crusaders:

So the man who inspired terror from the Mediterranean to the British sea fell by a blow from a single stone; at his fall those who had previously stood firm fell down.[9]

9 Sibley, W. A., and Sibly, M. D. (tr.) *The Chronicle of William of Puylaurens* (The Boydell Press: Woodbridge,) p. 61.

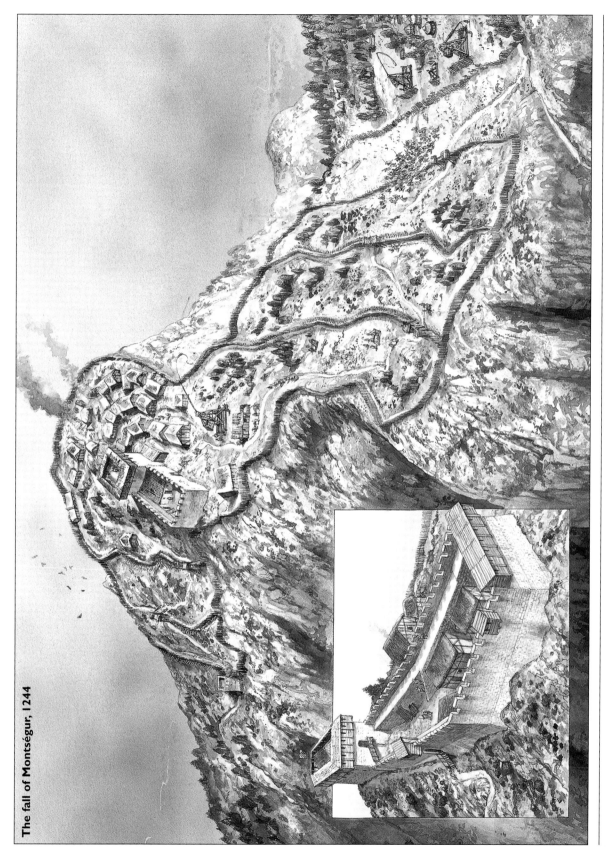

The fall of Montségur, 1244

Following the southern victory Prince Louis returned to the south in 1219, and attempted to besiege Toulouse; however, after 45 days of little progress he was forced to admit failure and returned to Paris. When Toulouse finally fell to the royal forces of France, it was not by siege but through treaties and marriage alliances.

Montségur, 1243–44

By the early 1240s the situation in the Languedoc was very different to how things had stood at the death of Simon de Montfort. His son, Amaury, had slowly lost the territories his father had won until he finally relinquished his claims to his various southern titles in 1224, making them all over to the French crown. By this stage Philip-Augustus had died and been succeeded by his son Louis VIII. Count Raymond VI of Toulouse had also passed away, succeeded by his son Raymond VII who pressed for his lands to be returned. In 1226 Louis VIII returned to the Languedoc, taking all the great towns of the south (bar Toulouse) before dying at Montpensier. His lieutenants continued the war and, by 1229, Raymond VII was forced to submit to both church and king by the Treaty of Paris. In 1240 Raymond-Roger of Trencavel made a vain attempt to win back his lands while Raymond VII also rebelled against the cruel conditions imposed by the Treaty of Paris. Both failed and in 1242 made their peace with the French crown – the last great rebellion in Languedoc had sputtered out and only isolated pockets of resistance remained.

This view shows the inside of the fortifications constructed at Montségur by Guy of Lévis II following the fall of the Cathar fortress. The two-storey keep is situated at the far end of the courtyard and a ladder to the first floor provides access to it. An arrow slit covers the interior of the courtyard. (Author's collection)

One of these was the fortress of Montségur, situated in the foothills of the Pyrenees to the south-east of Foix, which had become a centre of the Cathar faith. The site had been continuously occupied for over 1,000 years, but its most recent incarnation came following 1204 when the lord, Raymond of Pereille, had been asked by the Cathar Perfect to create a bastion there in case of trouble. The awaited trouble did indeed come and, following the submission of Raymond VII in 1229, a large number of the Cathar Perfect travelled there, including Guilhabert of Castres, Cathar bishop of Toulouse, along with other refugees from the conflict and their defenders. It has been estimated that by the time of the siege in 1243/44 there were over 400 inhabitants living in this isolated spot, under the command of Raymond of Pereille's son-in-law, Peter-Roger of Mirepoix.

Peter-Roger had been an important figure in the resistance to the northern crusade, losing his lands after the Treaty of Paris, and during the uprising of 1240–42 he, along with other knights from Montségur, had been among those responsible for the murder of two Catholic inquisitors in the town of Avignonet and the destruction of their records. Montségur was already known to the Catholic authorities as a place of refuge for Cathars, but this act made them even more determined to wipe it off the map.

In April 1243, once the final remnants of the revolt in the Languedoc had been put down, Hugh of Arcis, the royal seneschal in Carcassonne, assembled a large force and marched on Montségur. The exact number of men accompanying Hugh is unknown, but it was certainly thousands: figures of between 6,000 and 10,000 have been quoted in various sources. To face this threat the Cathar defenders had fewer than 100 soldiers – the Cathar Perfect could not fight and the rest of the inhabitants were women, children and the infirm.

Although the odds were heavily in the royal contingent's favour, the location of Montségur was a great leveller. The Cathar fortifications were situated on the top of a *pog* that could only sensibly be approached from the south-west, and this route was precipitous and well defended. Siege machines were useless in these situations as they did not have the range and elevation to hit the target. Hugh also lacked sufficient troops to surround the whole of the hill, so supplies could trickle into the besieged site from the surrounding villages. Montségur was well supplied with both provisions and water, possessing several wells, so there was no chance that thirst would drive the defenders out as it had in a number of the other sieges of the Albigensian Crusade.

The deadlock continued throughout the whole of the summer of 1243 and it was not until around Christmas that the Catholic forces achieved a breakthrough. At the north-eastern end of the *pog* was a defensive position situated on top of the Roc de la Tour, which itself rose up steeply from the valley floor. A group of Gascons managed to climb this precipitous slope by night – William of Puylaurens states that they would not have climbed it in daylight as it was so terrifying. They caught the defenders unawares, killed them, occupied the position and gained a vital toehold on the top of the mountain.

Now the royal army was able to start bringing its siege weapons up to the top of the mountain – piece by piece – to batter the defensive walls of Montségur; it was only a matter of time before the place would fall. It still managed to hold out for a further three months as the royal forces inched closer and closer to the central bastion of the site. Peter-Roger of Mirepoix attempted a sortie to drive the royal troops from the Roc and destroy their siege weapons, but it failed, and on 2 March 1244 he sought terms.

The terms were generous considering the length of the siege. Following a two-week period of truce all those present within Montségur were to be allowed to depart, with the soldiers even allowed to keep their arms. The only major condition was that they would have to submit to an interview with the Inquisition (founded in 1233 by Pope Gregory IX and closely associated with the Dominican order), and any self-confessed Cathars would have to recant their heresy and be reconciled with the Catholic Church.

The Cathar Perfect present at Montségur were no more inclined to renounce their beliefs than their predecessors at Minerve and the many other sites taken by the crusaders over the past 25 years. After their two-week period of grace over 200 of them walked down to the bottom of the hill, where they were burnt to death.

The only chronicler still describing the events at this stage, William of Puylaurens, relates the fall as follows:

> The defenders in the *castrum* were given no respite from attack by day or night … and abandoned to the attackers the *castrum* and the robed heretics who were found there, numbering about 230 men and women … The heretics were invited to accept conversion, but refused. They were confined to an enclosure made of pales and stakes. This was set on fire, they were burnt and passed onto the fire of Tartarus.[10]

Among those burnt were a number of soldiers and lay people who had been admitted to the Cathar faith following the surrender of the fortress, choosing to die as heretics rather than go free.

[10] Sibley, W. A., and Sibly, M. D. (tr.) *The Chronicle of William of Puylaurens* (The Boydell Press: Woodbridge,) p. 108.

Aftermath

Following the fall of Montségur, a number of isolated Cathar outposts managed to resist the French royal onslaught. Quéribus did not fall until 1255 and Usson held out till 1258; however, the inexorable advance of French royal control brought with it the apparatus of the Inquisition. In 1252 Pope Innocent IV promulgated the bull *Ad Extirpanda*, which allowed for the torture of suspects, giving the Inquisition another weapon in its armoury. Throughout the second half of the 13th century the Cathars became increasingly isolated and, by the early years of the 14th century, there were very few Perfect left to administer the *consolamentum* to the believers. Principal amongst the remaining Perfect were the Autier brothers, William and Peter, who were active around the turn of the century. Betrayed by a follower, William Autier was captured and burned in 1305, with his brother following him to the stake in 1310. This left only one recognized Cathar Perfect in the Languedoc, William Belibaste. When he was captured and burned at Villerouge-Termenès in 1321 the Cathar heresy in the Languedoc died too.

As far as the fortifications were concerned, they became part of the French frontier with Aragon following the Treaty of Corbeil in 1258. In 1250 Count Raymond VII of Toulouse died and his daughter Jeanne of Toulouse and her husband, Alphonse of Poitiers, brother of the king of France, inherited the County of Toulouse. Following Jeanne and Alphonse's deaths in 1271 the county was absorbed into the royal possessions according to the terms of the Treaty of Paris in 1229, placing the entire Languedoc directly under royal control.

This view from the medieval ramparts of the town shows the *castrum* of Saissac – consisting of the walled town and the castle – emphasizing its strategic position perched on the slopes of the Montagne Noire. Saissac played little part in the Albigensian Crusade, though its lord, Bertrand of Saissac, fought with Raymond-Roger Trencavel at the siege of Carcassonne in 1209. (Author's collection)

In the 14th century the region was affected by the Hundred Years' War, and Edward the Black Prince arrived outside Carcassonne in 1355 during his great *chevauchée* through the Languedoc. Although he destroyed the lower town, the defences of the *Cité* were so strong that he withdrew without attacking. Later, in the 16th century the region became a centre for the conflict known as the Wars of Religion and the Languedoc was a powerbase of the Protestant forces. Henry of Navarre, who eventually became Henry IV of France in 1593, was a descendant of the counts of Foix.

In 1659, the Treaty of the Pyrenees was signed between France and Spain to bring an end to a conflict that had its origins in the Thirty Years' War earlier in the century. By this treaty Louis XIV gained the territory of Roussillon along the Pyrenees, thus rendering the existing border fortifications of the Languedoc – including Carcassonne and its five sons – obsolete. To consolidate his new possessions Louis called upon his famed engineer Sebastien Le Prestre de Vauban to construct new fortifications in the region – particularly around the city of Perpignan and the newly constructed town of Mont-Louis, high in the Pyrenees. The Cathar castles were either converted into private residences or abandoned, a process that was accelerated with the French Revolution in 1789, when many of the fortifications were appropriated and sold by local committees.

In was not until the late 19th and 20th centuries that efforts were made to restore first the fortifications of Carcassonne and then some of the other distinctive monuments of the region. This renewed interest in the fortified sites coincided with a renewed interest in Catharism, and the 20th century has seen the Cathars adopted by many different group and ideologies.

In the late 19th century the French historian Napoleon Peyrat first popularized the myth of the treasure of Montségur – a fabulous hoard of untold wealth and mystic teachings that was removed from Montségur before it fell and taken to a place of safety. This idea was further developed throughout the 20th century, particularly by a German historian called Otto Rahn, who identified the Cathar treasure with the various Holy Grail myths, and had the Cathars, in particular Esclarmonde of Foix, being the guardians of the Holy Grail. Rahn's later work on the Cathars and racial purity (he was to join the Waffen-SS) have led to spurious associations between Nazism and Catharism, none of which have been proven. The notion of the Cathars as protectors of the Holy Grail was taken further in the book *The Holy Blood and the Holy Grail* by Michael Baigent, Richard Leigh and Henry Lincoln, a bestseller from the early 1980s. In it the authors assert that the Holy Grail is in fact the bloodline of Jesus Christ, descended from his marriage to Mary Magdalene. This has resurfaced in recent years with the publication of Dan Brown's novel *The Da Vinci Code* in 2003, one of the most widely read books of recent years, where it forms one of the key aspects of the plot.

Visiting the sites today

The Languedoc offers plenty of variety for the visitor, from the beaches of the Mediterranean coast, the rugged hill country of the Corbières, the great cities of Toulouse, Perpignan and Carcassonne, to the towering range of the Pyrenees to the south. It is increasingly easy to get there from the UK, with the larger airlines such as Air France and British Airways flying to Toulouse, as well as the low-cost carriers like EasyJet and Ryanair going to the smaller hubs such as Carcassonne and Perpignan. By road, the opening of the staggering Viaduct de Millais, designed by Sir Norman Foster, has reduced congestion on the main route south from Paris.

The summer months can be very busy in the region, when many of the major sites have extended opening hours well into the evening. The winter months, by contrast, see many of the Cathar Castles operating vastly reduced hours – often closed altogether apart from at weekends or on public holidays. The best time to visit the region is early or late summer, avoiding the French school holidays yet still getting the best of the weather.

For more information on the region there are a number of useful websites listed below, along with details of some of the major sites in the region:
www.cr-languedocroussillon.fr
www.payscathare.org
www.audetourisme.com
www.cathares.org
www.languedoc-france.info

Aguilar
The castle of Aguilar, one of the 'five sons of Carcassonne' is situated on an isolated hilltop, Mont Tauch, dominating the plain and village of Tuchan that lies below. It is just off the D611 from Durban-Corbières.
Open from 15 June to 15 September
1000–1230hrs and 1530–1900hrs
Contact : Mairie de Tuchan
BP 3 - 11350 Tuchan
Tel: 04 68 45 51 00
Fax: 04 68 45 49 97

Arques
The castle of Arques stands on the D613 about 14km to the east of the town of Couiza. The castle itself lies about 1,500m outside of the village, within which is located an exhibition on Catharism in the Maison de Deódat Roché.
Opening hours:
March, October, 1030–1200hrs, 1330–1730hrs
April, May, 1030–1830hrs
June, September, 1000–1900hrs
July, August, 0930–2000hrs
1–14 November, 1030–1200hrs, 1330–1700hrs
Closed from 15 November to the beginning of March
Contact: Château d'Arques
11 190 Arques
Tel/fax : 04 68 69 82 87
Email: site.arques@voila.fr

Carcassonne
The modern city of Carcassonne is divided into three sections: the medieval *Cité* standing high above the River Aude; the *Ville Basse* (historically known as

Carte Inter-Sites

Particularly useful for those visiting the Cathar sites of the Languedoc is the Carte Inter-Sites. This is a booklet costing 4 Euro that gives a 1 Euro discount on entrance to 18 of the most popular Cathar sites in the region. It covers the following locations:

Abbey of Saint-Papoul
Castle of Aguilar
Castle of Arques
Castle and walls of the Cité of Carcassonne
Abbey of Caunes-Minervois
Abbey of Fontfroide
Abbey of Lagrasse
Castle of Lastours
Castle of Peyrepertuse
Castle of Puilaurens
Museum of Quercorb at Puivert
Castle of Quéribus
Abbey of Saint-Hilaire
Castle of Saissac
Castle of Termes
Castle of Usson
Abbey of Villelongue
Castle of Villerouge-Termenès

The booklet itself is highly illustrated and available in multiple languages; it gives a brief history of each of the sites and the vouchers are valid for a year. It can be purchased at any of the participating sites, with the exception of the Cité of Carcassonne.

Although a castle at Arques is recorded from the beginning of the 11th century, the building that stands there today was constructed in the late 13th and early 14th centuries. The centrepiece of the structure consists of a 25m-high, four-storey rectangular keep with towers on each corner. (Author's collection)

the Bastide of St Louis); and the modern city that has grown up around them both. The medieval fortifications of Carcassonne are located in the *Cité* and can be accessed from the west via the Porte d'Aude or from the east via the Porte Narbonnaise.

Opening hours:

October–March, 0930–1700hrs

April–September, 0930–1800hrs

Closed on 1 January, 1 May, 1 November, 11 November and 25 December

Contact: Centre des monuments nationaux

Château et Rempart de la cité de Carcassonne

1, rue Viollet-le-Duc

11 000 Carcassonne

Tel: 04 68 11 70 72

Email: cite.carcassonne@monum.fr

Website: www.monum.fr

Lastours

The four castles of Lastours lie to the north of Carcassonne in the region known as the Montagne Noire. They are easily accessed from the D118, the main road from Carcassonne to Mazamet. There is a large visitor centre here, well equipped with pamphlets and books on the subject of the Cathars and the Albigensian Crusade.

Opening hours:

Closed in January

February, March, from 12 November to 31 December

    (weekends, school holidays and public holidays only) 1000–1700hrs

April–June, September, 1000–1800hrs

July and August, 0900–2000hrs

October–11 November, 1000–1700hrs

Contact: Châteaux de Lastours

11 600 Lastours

Tel/fax : 04 68 77 56 02

Email: chateaux.lastours@online.fr

Website: http://chateauxlastours.lwd.fr

Peyrepertuse

Peyrepertuse is one of the largest and best preserved of the Cathar castles. It is located a little way off the D117, the road from Perpignan to Quillan. It lies 4km north-west of the village of Cucugnan along the D14, within sight of the neighbouring castle of Quéribus.

Opening hours:
Closed in January
February, 1000–1730hrs
March, 1000–1800hrs
April, May, June, September, 0930–1900hrs
July and August, 0900–2000hrs
October, 1000–1830hrs
November and December, 1000–1700hrs
Contact: Château de Peyrepertuse
11 350 Duilhac-sous-Peyrepertuse
Tel (château): 06 71 58 63 36
Tel (mairie) : 04 68 45 40 55
Fax: 04 68 45 24 05
Email: chateau.peyrepertuse@wanadoo.fr
Website: www.château-peyrepertuse.com

Puilaurens

The castle of Puilaurens stands high above the village of Lapradelle-Puilaurens and lies just off the D117, the main route between Quillan and Perpignan.

Opening hours:
Closed the last three weeks of January
April–June, September, 0900–1900hrs
July, August, 0900–2030hrs
October, 1000–1800hrs
Contact: Château de Puilaurens
11 140 Lapradelle-Puilaurens
tel/fax: 04 68 20 65 26

ABOVE Heavily, and controversially, restored in the late 19th century, the fortifications of Carcassonne provide one of the major tourist attractions of the Languedoc. The interior of the fortifications houses a number of museums, as well as umpteen gift shops and restaurants. (Courtesy of Nikolai Bogdanovic)

OPPOSITE PAGE, BOTTOM RIGHT
The restored keep of Quéribus towers over the rest of the fortifications of the castle. The castle has been heavily restored over the last decade and is now a popular destination for tourists. (Author's collection)

Puivert

The castle of Puivert is located in the village of the same name about 20 minutes to the west of Quillan on the D117, the road to Foix. The Museum of Quercorb is situated in the same village and has displays of medieval instruments and other crafts.

Opening hours:
January–March; November–December: 1000–1700hrs
April–October, 0900–2000hrs
Contact: Michel Mignard – Château de Puivert
11230 Puivert
Tel/fax: 00 33 4 68 20 81 52
Email: infos@chateau-de-puivert.com
Website: www.chateau-de-puivert.com

Quéribus

Quéribus, situated within sight of the neighbouring fortress of Peyrepertuse, stands high up on the Grau de Maury. It can be easily reached from the Perpignan to Quillan road (D117) and is located just outside the village of Cucugnan on the D14.

Opening hours:
From 1 April to 18 June, 1100–1700hrs
From 19 June to 10 September, 1100–1900hrs
From 11 September to 12 November, 1100–1700hrs
Closed from mid-November to the end of March
Contact: Château de Quéribus
11 350 Cucugnan
Tel/fax: 04 68 45 03 69
Email: queribuscucugnan@wanadoo.fr
Website: www.queribuscucugnan.fr

ABOVE The fortress of Peyrepertuse as seen from the upper level of defences, the San Jordi. This higher level of fortification was constructed in the second half of the 13th century, at the same time as the lower level of fortifications was upgraded, to suit Peyrepertuse's new role as one of the bastions protecting the southern frontier of France. (Author's collection)

Termes

The castle of Termes is tucked away in the Corbières hills, standing above the small village of the same name. It is best reached by taking the D613 from Villerouge-Termenès and then the D40 to the village itself.

Opening hours:
Closed in January, February and December
March and from 16 October to 30 November,
    1030–1230hrs and 1330–1700hrs
April–June and September to 15 October,
    1030–1830hrs
July and August, 0930–2000hrs
Contact: Château de Termes
11330 Termes
Tel/fax: 04 68 70 09 20
Email: chateau.termes@wanadoo.fr

Usson

The castle of Usson, one of the last refuges of the Cathars, lies on the D118 south of Quillan, right at the centre of the Donezan region.

Although a number of the Cathar castles, such as Lastours, Montségur, Quéribus and Peyrepertuse, have been carefully restored over the years, the vast majority of the hilltop fortifications of the region still lie in a state of disrepair. The castle of Durfort, situated only 3km away from Termes, is typical of many of the fortifications of the area. (Author's collection)

Opening hours:
Closed from 16 November to 31 December
February and March (school holidays and weekends only), 1000–1630hrs
April–June, September, 1000–1730hrs
July and August, 0900–1930hrs
October to 15 November 0900–1930hrs
Contact: Château d'Usson
09 460 Rouze
Tel (château): 04 68 20 43 92
Tel (office de tourisme): 04 68 20 41 37
Fax: 04 68 20 46 25
Email: ot@donezan.com
Website: www.donezan.com

The castle of Usson is one of the more remote fortifications of the region, situated on the edge of the Pyrenees right on the far border of the County of Foix. Following the fall of Montségur in 1244 it served as refuge for the Cathar Perfect under its lords Bernard of Alion and Arnold of Usson. Bernard of Alion was burned at Perpignan in 1258. (Author's collection)

Villerouge-Termenès

The castle of Villerouge-Termenès is situated in the village of the same name south-west of Fontfroide along the D613. The castle contains an audiovisual history of William Belibaste, the last Cathar Perfect, who was burned here in 1321, as well as a *rôtisserie médiévale*, serving dishes from the Middle Ages.

Opening hours:
Closed in January
February, March, 16 October–31 December
    (weekends and public holidays only), 1000–1700hrs
April–June, September–15 October, 1000–1800hrs
July, August, 0930–1930hrs
Contact: Château
11330 Villerouge-Termenès
Tel (reception): 00 33 4 68 70 09 11 / 00 33 4 68 70 04 89
Fax: 00 33 4 68 70 04 37
Email: chateau.villerouge@wanadoo.fr

Very little remains of the fortifications of the town of Mirepoix, situated between Foix and Carcassonne, which were rebuilt in the late 14th century following a fire. The Porte d'Aval, shown here, is a square gate-tower dating from that period. During the Albigenisan Crusade Mirepoix was captured by Simon de Montfort and its lord disinherited. Peter-Roger of Mirepoix was later to play a pivotal role in the defence of Montségur. (Author's collection)

Further reading

There exists a considerable body of literature on the Cathars and the Albigensian Crusade in both French and English. For those with a reading knowledge of French, the acknowledged master of the subject is Michel Roquebert, who has written numerous books on the subject, including a title specifically on the castles: *Citadelles du Vertige*. The most prominent French historian writing on the subject at the moment is Anne Brenon, who has numerous published works to her name.

In recent years there have been a number of popular accounts of the Albigensian Crusade written in English, and two of the most approachable are Stephen O'Shea's *The Perfect Heresy* and Aubrey Burl's *God's Heretics*. All the major sources for the period – the *Chronicle of Peter of les Vaux-de-Cernay*, the *Chronicle of William of Puylaurens* and the *Song of the Cathar Wars* – are now available in print, the latter translated by Janet Shirley and the former two by W. A. and M. D. Sibly.

One final resource that it is essential to mention is the website www.cathares.org. This group of sites, run by the Histophile organization under Philippe Contal, contains a vast amount of information on the Cathars and the locations associated with them. It consists of a public portal and a private members-only area containing more in-depth material and is well worth joining for anyone seriously interested in the subject.

Barber, Malcolm, *The Cathars: Dualist Heretics in the Languedoc in the High Middle Ages*, Pearson Education Ltd: Harlow, 2000.

Bayrou, Lucien, L'Éperon de Peyrepertuse, *Archéologie du Midi Médiéval*, 1984, pp.194–99.

Bayrou, Lucien, *Peyrepertuse: Forteresse Royale*, Édition du Centre d'archéologie médiévale du Languedoc: Carcassonne, *c*. 2000.

Boussard, Jacques, *Atlas Historique et Culturel de la France*, Elsevier: Paris, 1957.

Brenon, Anne, *Le Vrai Visage du Catharisme*, Loubatieres: Portet-sur-Garonne, 1988.

Brenon, Anne, *Les Femmes Cathares*, Perrin: Paris, 1992.

Burl, Aubrey, *God's Heretics: the Albigensian Crusade*, Sutton Publishing Ltd: Stroud, 2002.

Corfis, Ivy A. and Wolfe, Michael, *The Medieval City under Siege*, The Boydell Press: Woodbridge, 1995.

Costen, M., *The Cathars and the Albigensian Crusade*, Manchester University Press: Manchester, 1997.

Geary, Patrick J., *Before France and Germany: The Creation and Transformation of the Merovingian World*, Oxford University Press: Oxford, 1988.

Le Roy Ladurie, Emmanuel, *Montaillou*, Penguin: Harmondsworth, 1980.

Martin, Sean, *The Cathars: The Most Successful Heresy of the Middle Ages*, Pocket Essentials: Harpenden, 2005.

McKitterick, Rosamund, *The Frankish Kingdoms under the Carolingians*, Longman: Harlow: 1983.

Mesqui, Jean, *Châteaux Forts et Fortifications en France*, Flammarion: Paris, 1997.

Nicolle, David, *Men-at-Arms 231: French Medieval Armies 1000–1300*, Osprey Publishing Ltd: Oxford, 1991.

Oldenbourg, Zoé, *Massacre at Montségur: a History of the Albigensian Crusade*, Weidenfeld and Nicolson: London, 1961.

O'Shea, Stephen, *The Perfect Heresy: The Life and Death of the Cathars*, Profile Books: London, 2001.

Poux, Joseph, *La Cité de Carcassonne: Précis Historique, Archéologique et Descriptif*, Edouard Privat: Toulouse, 1923.

Quehen, René, and Dieltiens, Dominique, *Les Châteaux Cathares et les autres*, (self-published) Toulouse, 1983.

Ritter, Raymond, *Châteaux, Donjons et Places Fortes: L'Architecture Militaire Française*, Librarie Larousse: Paris, 1953.

Roquebert, Michel, *Citadelles du Vertige*, Edouard Privat: Toulouse, 1966.

Roquebert, Michel, *L'Epopée Cathare*, 5 vols., Edouard Privat: Toulouse, 1970–89.

Salch, Charles-Lauren, *L'Atlas des Châteaux Forts en France*, Éditions Publitotal: Strasbourg, 1977.

Sarret, Jean-Pierre, La Communauté de Montségur au XIIIe siecle, *Archéologie du Midi Médiéval*, 1984, pp. 111–24.

Shirley, Janet (tr.), *Song of the Cathar Wars: a history of the Albigensian Crusade by William of Tudela and an anonymous successor*, Ashgate Publishing: Aldershot, 2000.

Sibly, W. A., and Sibly, M. D. (tr.), *The History of the Albigensian Crusade by Peter of les Vaux-de-Cernay*, The Boydell Press: Woodbridge, 1998.

Sibly, W. A., and Sibly, M. D. (tr.), *The Chronicle of William of Puylaurens*, The Boydell Press: Woodbridge, 2003.

Sumption, Jonathan, *The Albigensian Crusade*, Faber and Faber: London, 1999.

Warner, Philip, *Sieges of the Middle Ages*, Penguin: Harmondsworth, 1968.

Wolff, Philippe, *Histoire de Toulouse*, Edouard Privat: Toulouse, 1986.

Index